SPACE WARFARE
AND STRATEGIC DEFENSE

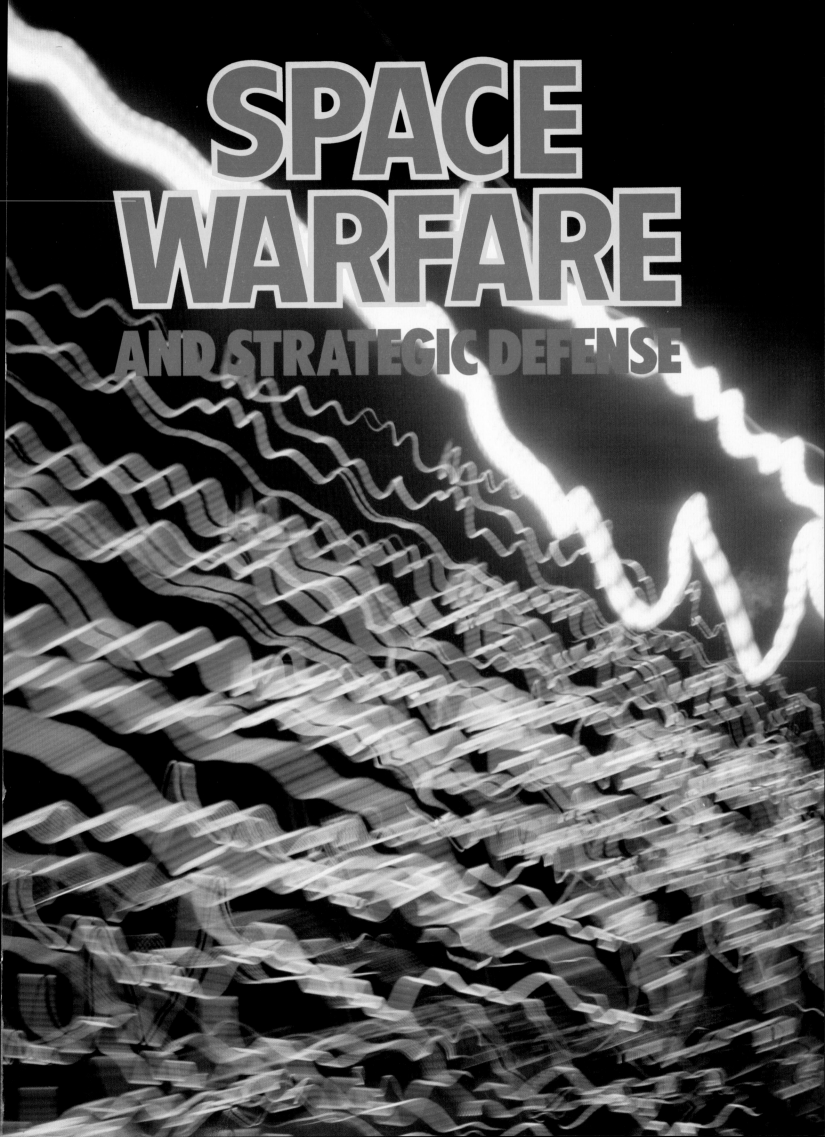

SPACE WARFARE

AND STRATEGIC DEFENSE

DAVID PAHL

Exeter Books

First Published in USA 1987
by Exeter Books
Distributed by Bookthrift
Exeter is a trademark of Bookthrift Marketing, Inc.
Bookthrift is a registered trademark of Bookthrift
Marketing, Inc.
New York, New York

ISBN 0-671-08925-0

Printed in Hong Kong

Designed by Ruth DeJauregui
Edited by John Kirk and Timothy Jacobs

Acknowledgements

We wish to thank the following people and organizations, who have contributed information and materials to make the completion of this book possible: Ken Carter and Ed Michalski of the United States Department of Defense; Mike Ross of Lawrence Livermore Laboratories; Bill Jack Rogers of Los Alamos National Laboratories; and Don Montoya of White Sands Missile Range.

Photo Credits

All photos courtesy of the United States Department of Defense except:
Bison Picture Library: 16 (left), 17 (top), 23 (bottom)
Ivar Blixti), Swedish Air Force: 22-23 (top)
Boeing: 12-13 (left), 35 (right), 36-37 (left), 37 (top right), 89, 156-157, 158
Peter Endsleigh Castle: 185 (bottom) (chart)
Master Sergeant Hiyashi: 163
Hughes Aircraft Company: 92
Imperial War Museum, London: 8
Lawrence Livermore National Laboratory: 127 (bottom), 131, 136, 138
Los Alamos National Laboratory: 72 (left), 74, 123 (right), 126, 129 (top and bottom), 130, 134, 135, 168, 169, 180 (bottom), 181
McDonnell Douglas Corporation: 42-43 (all), 67
NASA: 2-3, 7, 90 (left), 93, 99, 192
Rockwell International: 38-39, 41, 56-57, 90-91 (right), 160
Smithsonian Institution: 133
Sperry: 116
James E Stoots, Jr: 180 (top)
TASS: 22, 31
Ullstein: 9
United States Air Force: 10 (upper left), 15, 18-19 (left), 21, 25 (bottom), 34-35 (left), 37 (bottom right), 45, 49, 50, 59 (top), 75, 80, 84, 86-87, 98, 101, 102, 103, 106 (left and right), 107, 108-109, 122-123 (left), 148-149, 151, 166, 170, 172, 173 (top), 178 (bottom), 183, 186 (bottom left and top right), 187 (left), 189, 191
United States Air Force, Buster Kellum: 104-105
United States Army: 48 (left and right), 58 (left and right), 83 (right), 184 (right), 188

White Sands: 4-5, 82-83 (left), 88, 125 (top and bottom), 153 (top and bottom), 154 (all), 155 (bottom left and right)
Wide World Photos: 14, 17 (bottom), 44
© Bill Yenne: 54 (chart), 68, 69, 100, 161, 164-165, 185 (top)

Page 1: A veritable blizzard of electronic rays seems to bury the viewer, evoking what most of us think of when we hear the words 'space warfare.'

Pages 2-3: Is this an unimaginably huge explosion of superhot gases enveloping the Earth and all she knows? Or is this an Iowa farmer's last look upward at the impossible bloom of a high atmospheric nuclear blast on a previously calm June evening? Though the Great Nebula in the Orion constellation is eternities of Earth time distant from us, its vast array of gaseous, primal stellar material recalls the seeming chaos of origin, and reminds us that, with fission and fusion weapons, the nuclear age has brought the heretofore *extraterrestrial* apparatus of stars to dwell on the face of our planet.

Below: This is a portion of the vast White Sands Missile Range in New Mexico, which has been the proving ground for many of our short and long range space age weaponry and includes laser weapons testing facilities. The first atomic bomb detonation occurred on the White Sands Missile Range on 16 July 1945, one week after the range was opened, at the Manhattan Project's 'Trinity' Site. The bomb, a model of which is on display at White Sands, was called 'Fat Man.'

CONTENTS

THE BASIS FOR THE STRATEGIC DEFENSE INITIATIVE

In March of 1983, the president of the United States announced a research and development project which, he said, 'holds the promise of changing the course of human history.' This project, called the Strategic Defense Initiative, would, according to the president, offer 'peace and a new hope for our children in the twenty-first century.' Not since President Kennedy's challenge to put astronauts on the moon has a president asked for so much from the scientific community. But what exactly is the Strategic Defense Initiative, and how does it change the world?

The Strategic Defense Initiative is a program of vigorous research focused on advanced defensive technologies with the aim of finding ways to provide a better basis for deterring aggression, strengthening stability, and increasing the security of the United States and our allies. The purpose of the research is to identify ways to exploit recent advances in ballistic missile defense technologies. The program is designed to answer a number of fundamental scientific and engineering questions that must be addressed before the promise of these new technologies can be fully assessed.

To have a better understanding of the Strategic Defense Initiative concept, we must first clearly understand the supposed need for such a defense. The program was plainly aimed at the Soviet Union and presented a deep-rooted fear of Soviet aggression and coercion.

There is a long history of mistrust and mutual suspicion between the Soviet Union and the United States. Indeed, there is really mistrust between every Soviet-supported country worldwide and the United States and its allies. Much of this distrust lies deeply rooted in political philosophy. The basic tenets of Russian communism condemn capitalistic systems of government in clearly moral terms. According to the philosophy, the capitalists ignore the needs of the individual by allowing some to have unfair advantage (through freer access to money) over others. At the core of Russian communism is world revolution. The people will struggle against oppression until they rise up and form a completely classless society. Because the United States is such a successful example of the capitalistic way of life, the Soviet focus is to 'convert' the people of America to the communist way of life.

On the other hand, the United States system tries to 'convert' people in communist systems away from their government's philosophy—on the presumption that if given freedom to choose, people everywhere will embrace a more democratic society. Clearly, the pressure from both sides to change the system of the other has led to animosity, if not downright dislike and antagonism.

More than philosophical differences affect the relationship between the Soviets and the western allies. Russia felt isolated and forgotten in the latter half of the 1930s. Hitler's

Above: US President Ronald Reagan, in a 23 March 1986 statement on the SDI, said that the project 'has been a singularly effective instrument in bringing the Soviets to the [arms reduction] bargaining table.' Critics call it 'Pie in the Sky,' and 'Star Wars.'

war machine was intimidating the Western European nations into giving up European territory in the faint hope that Germany would not attack. These Western attempts at appeasing Hitler caused the Soviets to be particularly concerned, if not completely suspicious, of what the Allied Forces would do if Hitler demanded territory that was all or a portion of Russia. Even though the political philosophies of Germany and Russia were opposed, the Soviets considered that their best option was to divert, somehow, the German attention away from their eastern border. As a result, in August of 1939, the Germans and Russians signed an agreement of strict neutrality.

Although the Soviets simply wanted to avoid war with Germany, the neutrality pact defined 'spheres of influence.' In effect, these spheres of influence gave the Soviets claim to all territory within their 'sphere' and they were quick to expand into Eastern Europe. The Red Army occupied Eastern Poland. Estonia, Latvia and Lithuania were 'incorporated' in 1940, and the Soviets obtained leases on key Baltic Sea bases. To this day, the United States does not recognize these three countries as being part of the Soviet Union. By the spring of 1940 the USSR had annexed Finland and, later that year, a portion of Rumania.

The 1939 neutrality pact shocked the Western European nations. Russia became an enemy in the minds of many—especially when the Soviets took advantage of the spheres of influence portions of the pact to annex new territory.

History would certainly have been different if Hitler had not decided to attack the Russians. In all likelihood those two countries would have eventually gone to war. However, that war would have been years off. As it was, the Russians were attacked and pushed back to the threshold of Moscow before they were able to slow and stall the relentless German attack. The valiant conduct of the Russian people in those dark days won the sympathy of the world. Even the Russian occupation of their 'sphere of influence' territory was forgotten for a time as the world praised the determination of the Russians and the defense of their homeland.

The valiant conduct of the Russian people and the sympathy left over from Hitler's surprise attack gave Stalin significant political prestige with the various Allied governments. He was able to capitalize on that prestige in post war agreements by demanding that friendly political regimes be established in the countries on Russia's western borders (it is likely that free elections in most of those Eastern European countries at the time would have resulted in anti-Soviet gov-

ernments). Through these demands, Stalin was able to control Poland, Bulgaria, Rumania, Hungary and East Germany. This sweeping Soviet expansion into Western Europe occurred, at least in part, because of the rapid withdrawal and demobilization of the Allied Forces.

Between 1945 and 1950, while the United States and the Allies were celebrating the great victory, the Russians continued to think about military strength. The attitude of the Western Allies was that the war was over so it was time to send the troops home; it was time to scrap or lay up warships and aircraft; it was time to forget military research and development. In those years of celebration and disarmament, the Soviet Union launched crash build-up programs in nuclear weapons design and rocketing. They also vastly expanded their submarine and surface warfare fleets. In addition, the Communist Party outside the Eastern Bloc tried to exploit (although unsuccessfully) their new prestige and win control of Western European governments. Although the war was over, the tension in the world remained at a high level.

Hope that the wartime alliance between the Soviets and the West would prosper after the war withered, as Stalin crushed and thoroughly dominated Russia's neighboring countries. Widespread arrests for political activities were common as Stalin 'climatized' these countries to their new government. This heavy-handed treatment by the security conscious Stalin prompted actions by Westerners. In 1947 the US adopted the Truman Doctrine of Containment of Soviet Expansion and provided both military and economic aid to the neighbors of the USSR. These were the governments whose independence was threatened directly or indirectly by the Communist state. The Marshall Plan was also adopted in 1947 and offered to underwrite the recovery of Europe. Because the Soviet Union and its satellites would not participate, the plan became a rallying point and a bond for the West.

Both of these actions were aimed specifically at containing the perceived Russian threat. Obviously, the Soviet Union viewed these actions as initial maneuvers which would ultimately mean war. The 1949 North Atlantic Treaty Or-

ganization (which established a permanent defensive force in Western Europe to protect against Soviet aggression) was no doubt the final straw for the Russians. If they had any reason to believe that they could eventually form some sort of alliance with the West, that hope was clearly gone. The battle lines, so to speak, were drawn and the Soviets clearly felt encircled. More importantly perhaps, the NATO alliance probably also brought the realization to the Russian leadership that the people of the other countries of the world were not going to revolt and take the theory of communism to heart. NATO showed that the USSR was not the irresistible model for world government.

The balance of power, at that point, remained on the side of the West. The United States was the only owner of nuclear arms. But when the Soviets successfully tested a nuclear device in August of 1949, the balance shifted and the arms race began. Many believe that this was a key time for the world. Because the Soviets felt increasingly 'hemmed in' by antagonists, it is likely that they felt compelled to prepare their arsenals for the war that was surely inevitable. There

was another consideration for the start of the arms race. If the Soviets could not 'convert' the people of the world to communism, they could command the respect of those same people by becoming the world's leading military power. The Russians began an unprecedented buildup of their armed forces.

At the time, the Soviet Army was not much more than a brute force group which was capable of winning only by overwhelming an enemy with superior numbers. Their navy was little more than a coastal fleet, and their air force was almost nonexistent. Realizing their frustration at being encircled by NATO and their inability to convert the people of the world, the Soviet leaders were no doubt delighted when they finally achieved nuclear power status. Their confidence in their military strength no doubt improved tremendously.

Above: A 'Little Boy' fission bomb of the type used in the bombing of Hiroshima. This bomb's yield was equivalent to 12,500 tons of TNT. *At right:* A US tactical nuclear test in Nevada, sometime in the early 1950s. The mushroom cloud image entered the public consciousness via news, entertainment and propaganda.

Indeed, many scholars believe that the outbreak of the Korean War in 1950 was instigated by the Soviets. Western governments at the time certainly believed that the undeclared war was a Soviet-sponsored initiative that grew out of the Russian leaders' new nuclear confidence. More ominously, Western leaders viewed this effort as a Russian strategic feint to draw the limited conventional forces of NATO (particularly the United States) to Korea while the Soviets prepared to invade Western Europe. This fear of a possible Russian attack on Western Europe stopped the demobilization of the Western Allied Forces. In fact, from the outbreak of the Korean War in 1950 until a peace accord was signed in 1954, the United States and the United Kingdom built up their forces. The steady build-up of Soviet strength was overtaken by the arming efforts of the West. However, as soon as the peace accords were signed, the West relaxed and went back to their peacetime pursuits. The Soviets, however, continued to build up their armed forces.

During the 1950s there was a story circulated about a fictional 'Doomsday Machine.' This machine was, so the story goes, a huge nuclear device which was so powerful that it could destroy the earth. This Doomsday Machine was designed to explode if any nation used nuclear weapons to attack another nation. According to the story, the Doomsday Machine was an effective peacekeeper because all nations understood that they would be committing suicide if they attacked with nuclear devices—even if the attack were successful, the Doomsday Machine would explode and destroy the earth.

By 1965, a short twenty years after the first man-made atomic explosion, there were enough nuclear weapons in arsenals around the world to make the Doomsday Machine story a reality. Ironically, the story line for the fictional tale had, in a way, become the basis for a tenuous peace between so-called world super powers. Mutually Assured Destruction (MAD) had replaced the Doomsday Machine as the theme for peaceful coexistence. In effect, MAD meant: 'If you fire at me, I will retaliate swiftly and heavily. I may be dead after the exchange, but then, so will you.'

The MAD philosophy fairly well insured that no nation would fire nuclear weapons at another without fear of equal and fearsome retribution. The arms race became a push to shift the balance of power by way of numerical advantage; to own such a superior arsenal of weapons that an enemy would fear that retribution may not be possible—in other words, to

have an arsenal of such overwhelming power that the threat of attack would cause a lesser nation to surrender without an exchange of nuclear weapons. The promise of 'nuclear blackmail' became the way to beat the mutually assured destruction strategy.

The original delivery systems for nuclear weapons were aircraft. The early weapons were awkward and quite heavy. By the 1960s there was a variety of methods by which to deliver atomic weapons. These included aircraft, cannon and missiles. Particularly worrisome for both sides were missiles. Technology had improved to a point where it was possible to hit targets anywhere in the world, either from permanent landbased missiles or from submarines operating off the coasts of a potential enemy.

Interestingly, by 1965 the United States still had a tremendous advantage over the Soviet Union in the area of landbased intercontinental ballistic missiles. At the time, the United States had assembled an arsenal of more than 800 such craft; more than four times the inventory of the Soviets. The American missiles were also quite accurate, while those of the Soviets were considered inaccurate and probably obsolete before they were even deployed. The Russian answer to the inaccuracy of their ICBMs was basically simple: build bigger warheads. The thinking here was that even if it missed its objective, the power of the nuclear warhead would still destroy its intended target.

The American advantage dwindled rapidly after 1965, however. During the years of our war in Viet Nam, military spending for strategic weaponry was cut and funneled into conventional forces. Further, because that war was not a popular one here at home, even the budgets for conventional arms were cut. All the while the Soviet Union continued to increase their spending in military arms and equipment. By 1970 the Soviets had acquired more than 1400 ICBMs of five warrior types. Admittedly, some portions of these weapons were old and probably obsolete, but they could still be used in an attack and, therefore, still counted as a major threat.

In 1975 the Russian ICBM force had reached just about 1600 missiles. Many of these were advanced and reasonably accurate weapons. The force included missiles designated the SS-17, SS-18, and SS-19, and all had multiple warhead capability. Toward the end of the 1970s the Soviet ICBM force declined to about 1400 missiles, but this decline merely reflected the greater accuracy, throw weight and warhead efficiency of the newer missiles.

The effectiveness of a ballistic missile is really described, first, in terms of accuracy of the warhead. The early Soviet missiles were not particularly accurate and could usually be expected to land somewhere within approximately two miles of their intended target. As a point of reference, American missiles of the day were capable of touching down within ap-

proximately 100 yards of their objective. To make up for this inaccuracy, the Soviets installed huge warheads to destroy their objective even if the warhead missed its mark. The later model missiles greatly improved the accuracy of the Soviet missiles. Indeed, they were able to touch down within approximately 250 yards of their objectives. Interestingly, even though the accuracy improved, the Russians continued to utilize very large warheads. This was of particular concern to United States military planners because the accuracy and size of the Russian warheads were such that they could destroy an American missile silo, along with associated personnel and support equipment, from as far away as 250 yards. The Soviets, by the late 1970s, had the capability to destroy 70–75 percent of the US Minuteman missile sites in a surprise attack.

'Throw weight' refers to the capability of the missile to deliver a payload to a target. The greater the weight of a warhead (or the greater the number of warheads a missile must lift), the greater the missile's throw weight capability. The Soviet SS-18 missile is certainly a case in point. The SS-18 has a throw weight which is more than twice that of the now obsolete US Titan II, the largest missile in the American fleet. The SS-18 is easily the largest and most powerful ICBM in the world. It can carry a single nuclear warhead with an estimated power of about 30 megatons. Configured differently, the SS-18 can have a multiple warhead capability which

The B-29 Superfortress *Enola Gay (above left)* dropped the 'Little Boy' bomb on Hiroshima in 1945, causing massive destruction and killing tens of thousands of people. *Above:* The test launching of a Douglas SM-75 Thor IRBM by the USAF in the late 1950s.

At right: A Peacekeeper LGM-118 'MX' missile blasts upward in an explosive cloud from the launch facility at Warren Air Force Base. Above: A Soviet T-55 tank rumbles through Czechoslovakian streets during the Czech resistance in 1968.

varies with the size of the warhead—the SS-18 can be loaded with up to 30 warheads which are smaller than one megaton. We will hear more about the huge SS-18 later.

The United States was plainly concerned about the growth of Soviet military strength. By the late 1960s, the Johnson administration had set the stage for a hoped-for end to the seemingly uncontrolled growth of offensive weapons. The foundation for the Strategic Arms Limitation Talks (SALT) was laid prior to the end of President Johnson's term in office. However, the promised talks were delayed because of the tumultuous 1968 presidential campaign and the more serious Soviet invasion of Czechoslovakia. It was some time before newly-elected President Nixon would continue with the SALT effort. In the meantime, the arms race continued, but it seemed clear that the problem of deterrence could be beaten by developing an effective missile defense system.

The concern about defensive systems grew rapidly. It was clear that the balance of power would shift radically if one power were able to come up with an effective defensive system. Further, the push toward defenses only seemed to escalate the build-up of nuclear weapons. The thinking was

obvious: the only way to beat a missile defense system is to overwhelm it with a tremendous number of offensive weapons.

By the beginning of the 1970s, the leaders of the USSR and the US came to believe that the best opportunity for peace was when each side was able to threaten retaliation against any attack—and thereby impose on an aggressor costs which were well beyond any possible potential gains. This belief led to the 1972 Anti-Ballistic Missile (ABM) Treaty which placed definite limits on Russian and American defenses against ballistic missiles. This treaty said in part, that both powers:

- would limit anti-ballistic missile systems. ABM facilities were limited to deployment around a national capital and near any area with intercontinental ballistic missiles (ICBMs).
- would not develop, test or deploy ABM systems which are seabased, airbased, spacebased or mobile land-based.
- would not deploy radars for the early warning of a strategic ballistic missile attack, except at locations along the periphery of national territory (and that they be oriented outward).
- would allow technical verification of systems and would not deliberately conceal such systems in order to impede the verification.

Above : Soviet paratrooper training includes mock attacks on enemy missile sites. *Right :* Soviet soldiers in germ-proof anti-radiation suits. *Far right:* A rare photo of a Soviet ICBM in its silo. *Below right:* Presidents Carter and Brezhnev after signing SALT II in 1979.

The basic concept was that stability through deterrence could be maintained if each side had roughly equal capability to retaliate against attack. This premise became the basis for the Strategic Arms Limitation Talks (SALT) of the 1970s.

President Nixon pressed on with the SALT talks, and by the time he was succeeded by Gerald Ford, SALT II was a work well under way. In an effort to keep up the effort on the project during the post-Watergate turmoil, President Ford and Soviet Premier Brezhnev signed an accord in November of 1974. This accord did not produce a treaty, but did serve well as an intention. It would be a long time before the second SALT accord would be agreed upon and signed. SALT II was formally signed by the Carter administration in 1979.

SALT accords and the ABM treaty notwithstanding, according to the US Government, the Soviet Union has ignored the spirit of the treaties. Indeed, the Soviets have escalated their buildup of offensive nuclear weapons and at the same time have greatly improved their strategic defenses. The obvious concern about this development is that the balance of power will shift in favor of Russia. Further, if the Soviet Union developed an effective anti-ballistic missile defense, the Russian leaders would come to believe that a nuclear attack could be launched against the United States and its allies without fear of effective retaliaton. Even if there were no launch, the possibility for global blackmail would be real.

To the great concern of the West, during the last 20 years the Soviets have increased their active and passive defenses in a clear effort to diminish the effect of US and its allies' retaliation against an attack. Passive defenses are not weapons-oriented. These defenses focus on civil defense (air and missile shelters for the population) and hardening (building bunkers, in effect to protect valuable military resources). Physical hardening of military assets to make them more resistant to attack is an important passive defensive technique. The Soviet Union has hardened its ICBM silos, launch facilities and key command and control centers.

As a matter of concern for the West, much of the current US retaliatory force would be ineffective against those hardened targets.

At the same time, the USSR has expanded its offensive capability. During the past 15 years, the Soviet Union has built five new classes of intercontinental ballistic missiles (ICBMs). Further, they have upgraded these missiles at least seven times. As a result, their offensive missile force is considerably more powerful and more accurate than it was several years ago. As a basis for comparison, the United States introduced its last new intercontinental ballistic missiles, the Minuteman III and Minuteman IV in 1969 and 1974 respectively. The Minuteman system has been upgraded once in that period. The growth in quantity and quality of Soviet ballistic missile systems has the effect of significantly degrading US landbased retaliatory capability.

Indeed, at this point, the most important weapon in the arsenal of the Soviet Union is their collective force of land-based intercontinental ballistic missiles. A recent report showed that the USSR had more than 300 of the huge SS-18 missiles deployed. In addition, the Soviets also had nearly 400 SS-19 missiles which are comparable to the United States MX missiles. The fleet of SS-18 and SS-19 missiles can carry more than 5000 warheads, each with a capability of coming within about 300 yards of their targets. The SS-19, although smaller than the SS-18, can carry a single five megaton warhead or as many as six 50 kiloton warheads in the MIRV version. Finally, both of these large ICBM's can be 'cold launched'; that is, the missile is ejected out of its silo prior to the ignition of the rocket engines. This method of launch limits the blast damage to silo structures and allows the launch pads to be reloaded several times.

The Soviet Union also has a slightly shorter-range missile, the SS-20, in its inventory of strategic arms. The SS-20 is particularly worrisome as it is mounted on a mobile missile carrier which allows the craft to be hidden and makes arms verification very difficult. The SS-20 also has excellent range for an intermediate-range missile. Depending on how it is configured, each can carry as many as three warheads. The SS-20 has a range of better than 3000 miles. A recent count showed that the Soviet Union had at least 400 SS-20 launch-

Above: A Soviet SS-X-14 missile rises into launch position on its mobile launch platform. *At left:* This Boeing 'Minuteman' SM-80 ICBM is shown as installed in its silo just minutes before its test launch at the Kennedy Space Center at Cape Canaveral, Florida, on 7 January 1963.

ers, each with the capability of up to five reloads (six missile launches in total). Keeping in mind that each missile can carry up to three warheads, this means that the fleet of SS-20 launchers can deliver more than 7200 nuclear warheads in a conflict. Add this capability to the 5000 warheads carried by the SS-18s and SS-19s, and this portion of the Soviet missile fleet has tremendous destructive power.

Just prior to President Reagan's famous 'Star Wars' speech, the Soviets tested still another ICBM. Dubbed the SS-X-25, this missile was a solid fuel three-stage craft. Most importantly, the missile was mobile which would give the Soviet Union the capability to hide their intercontinental ballistic missile fleet. The Russians could then gain a significant strategic advantage because, by hiding the missiles or at least moving them around, they could ensure the survivability of its offensive force.

In all, since 1966 the Soviet Union has deployed not quite 1400 ICBMs. (These include the following missile types: SS-11, SS-13, SS-17, S-18, and SS-19.) If we assume that all

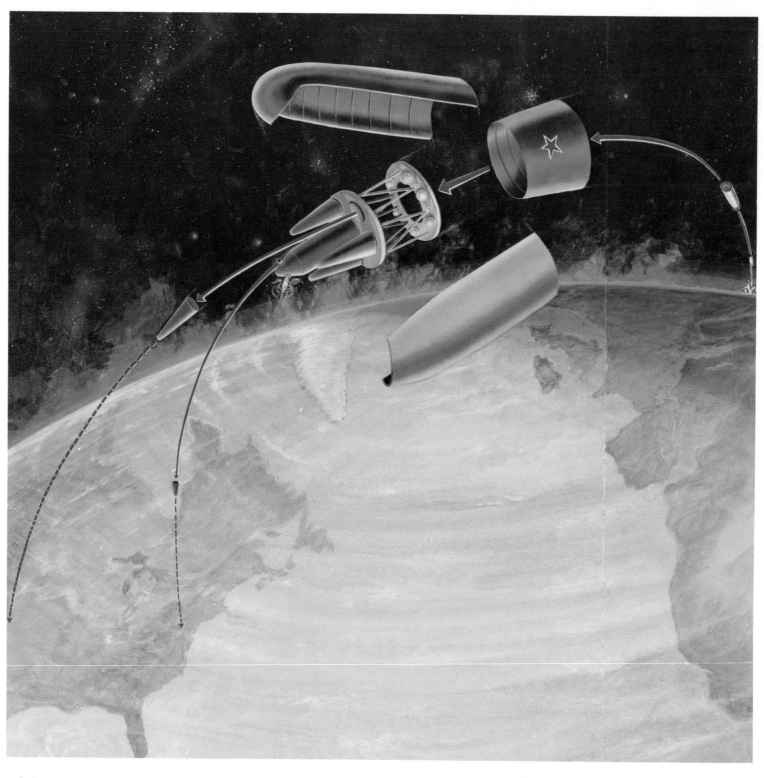

of these are loaded for maximum range and with multiple warheads, a conservative estimate of their explosive power is in the order of four billion tons of TNT—and this does not consider the possibility of reloading the weapons launchers, nor does it consider the relative long-range threats of SS-20s and other intermediate-range ballisitic missiles. For comparison purposes, the United States intercontinental ballistic missile fleet consists of slightly more than 1000 craft. Including the multiple warhead capability, these missiles represent a destructive equivalent of about 1.3 billion tons of TNT.

Looking to the future, the United States plans to eliminate the Titan missile from the fleet and fully deploy the MX with multiple warheads. On the Soviet side, reported plans include an MX class missile, the SS-X-24, the mobile SS-X-25 already discussed, and a large ICBM designated the SS-X-26.

A major threat is the Multiple Independent Reentry Vehicle warhead, which is shown from 'birth' to 'death' in the artist's impression *above*. A 10-story tall Titan II missile (*right*) stands waiting in its silo; its speed is 17,000mph; its range is 6300 miles.

The spectacular growth of Soviet military power, the result of an arms build-up which is unprecedented and the build-up of weapons from a destructive power standpoint is far greater than the Allied Forces mobilization for World War II.

Although not a missile build-up, the Russian government has also undertaken an almost unbelievable expansion of its conventional forces. Today's army, for instance, is different from the brute force assemblage of undrilled and unskilled soldiers of the late 1940s and early 1950s. Better equipped than even the armies of West Germany and the United States, the Soviet Army can deploy families of weapons,

Above: The Mach 2.3-capable Soviet MiG-23 'Flogger G' interceptor carries a variety of armament, and has radar 'look down' capability for detecting low-flying cruise missiles. *Below left:* T-72 tanks parade Soviet military might in Moscow's Red Square. *Right:* An SA-2 missile of the type that shot down Francis Gary Powers' U-2 in 1960.

vehicles and troop operations which offer the advantage of overlapping capabilities. Their army is well drilled and disciplined, capable of prolonged offensive effort, and capable of outmaneuvering any opponent. The Soviet Army is truly a superior force on the ground. It can combine the operational tactics of the famous German Army of early World War II, as well as the overwhelming numbers of soldiers typical of Russian armies throughout history. Finally, the Soviet Army by its very size and obvious superior equipment is a very threatening force for NATO countries to consider. These same qualities make the Soviet Union almost impregnable to a ground offensive by NATO.

By the 1980s the Soviet arsenal of equipment—both conventional and nuclear—has grown to the point where it exceeds the combined inventories of all of NATO (including the United States) and the People's Republic of China. This includes every category of military equipment except total surface ships and some small arms. Although Western equipment is arguably still of higher quality than Soviet items, the quantity of Russian goods more than makes up for any disparity in quality. With this in mind and ignoring the Soviet nuclear missile threat, the size and quality of the Russian conventional force is such that their military leaders would likely be capable of advancing through the NATO defenses almost with impunity. With regard to the quality of Soviet equipment, there is no doubt that the West has the edge on

the Soviets—but even with this advantage, the Russians catch up in their very quick production cycles. The Soviets have the remarkable capability to push technology advancements through to manufacture much faster than can their American counterparts.

For almost 20 years, United States military planners and some political leaders watched worriedly as the Soviets slowly caught up to America. The losing of the arms race ironically was by design. Some historians believe that it was the philosophy of 'Mutually Assured Destruction' which led to this losing of the arms race. For the United States, MAD

Above: MiG-21s sweep across the sky above a Soviet air defense radar antenna. The Soviet Anti Ballistic Missile radar network is illustrated in the diagram shown at *extreme upper right. At right:* An artist's conception of NASA's Navstar satellite constellation.

was really nonmilitary spending. The idea was that we could let the Russians spend a large fortune trying to catch up with the technically superior Americans. Probably, most doubted that the Soviets could catch up and, no doubt most believed that they would go broke in their futile attempt to catch up. For the United States, the MAD philosophy was compelling: the Russians spent vast amounts while the Americans spent almost nothing. While the United States sat back and saved money, the Soviet Union was allowed to acquire equipment and advantages in nearly every important strategic offensive category. As compelling as was the idea of allowing the Soviets to spend a fortune while we saved, the military planners were right to worry.

Unlike the Americans, the Russians were not only interested in offensive might. For over two decades the Soviet Union has pursued a wide range of strategic defensive efforts, including advanced anti-ballistic missile research and development.

By the mid-1960s, the Soviets focused on the development of two defense technologies—anti-satellite and anti-missile systems. In spite of the 1972 ABM Treaty, the Russians

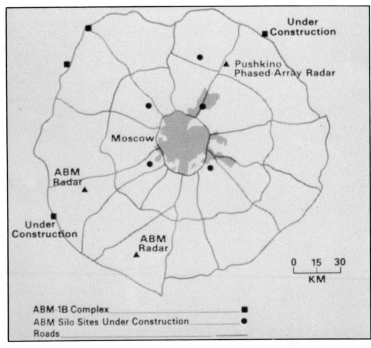

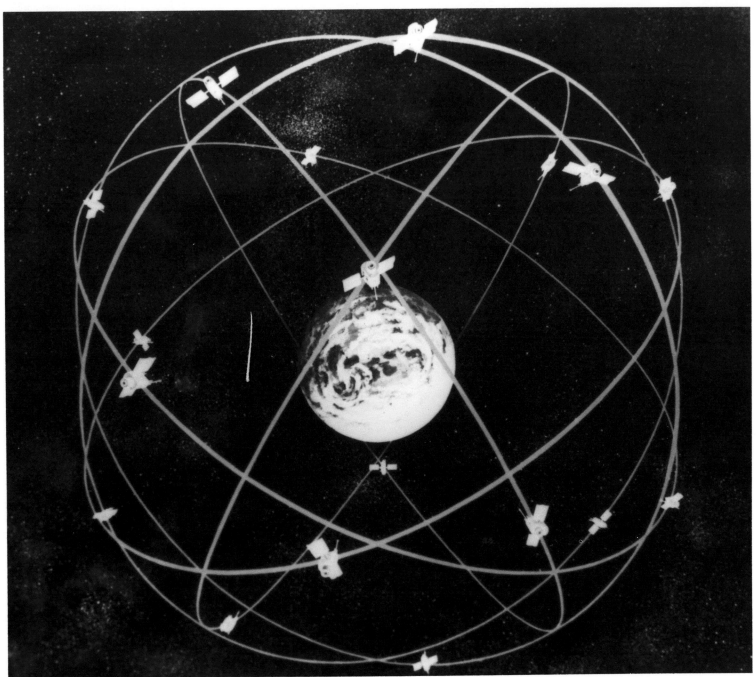

Soviet Territorial Air Defense

Interceptor aircraft bases _____ •

Strategic SAM concentrations _____ ▮

32

A US Department of Defense color diagram outlines the Soviet national air defense system *at left. Above left:* This is a rare photo of a now-obsolete Soviet Galosh ABM, 64 of which were positioned to protect Moscow. *Above:* The Soviets love to parade their weapons. *Here,* shorter-range mobile ICBM SS-X-15s are on parade in Red Square.

pressed on with their development of these defensive systems. As a result, the Soviet Union has the only operational anti-satellite (ASAT) system. This system is estimated by US analysts to have an effective capability to seek and destroy critical US satellites in a low earth orbit. Additionally, the Soviet efforts to develop a viable strategic defense against ballistic missiles has resulted in a large and expanding research and development program to enhance their operational ABM system.

The Soviet emphasis on the necessity of research into defenses against ballistic missiles was demonstrated by the then-Minister of Defense Grechko shortly after the 1972 ABM Treaty. Minister Grechko told the Soviet Presidium that the treaty 'places no limitations whatsoever on the conducting of research and experimental work directed towards solving the problem of defending the country from nuclear missile strikes.'

In 1980 the Soviets began to upgrade and expand their ABM system (surrounding Moscow) to the limit allowed by the ABM Treaty. The original single-layer system included 64 reloadable above-ground launchers at four separate complexes plus battle management radars south of Moscow. Each complex consisted of tracking and guidance radars and nuclear-armed groundbased missiles designed to intercept warheads in space shortly before they re-enter the Earth's atmosphere.

When completed, the modernized Moscow ABM system will be a two-layer defense composed of the system presented above plus silo-based, high-acceleration interceptors designed to engage targets within the atmosphere, associated engagement and guidance radars, and a new large radar to control ABM engagements. The enhanced system will have the 100 ABM launchers permitted by the ABM Treaty and could be fully operational by 1987.

The Soviet system for detection and tracking of a ballistic missile attack consists of a launch detection satellite network, over-the-horizon radars, and a series of large phased-array radars.

The current Russian launch detection satellite network can provide about 30 minutes warning of any US ICBM and determine the general origin of the missile. Since orbiting spacecraft have specific orbit characteristics, such as altitude and inclination to the Equator, it is possible in most cases to determine the actual purpose of the majority of Soviet satellites by examining the published data about the shape of the orbits.

Three Soviet satellite systems are of particular interest to US defense planners—RORSAT, EORSAT, and MOLNIYA. RORSAT and EORSAT are known to be used to track American naval movements, particularly carrier task forces. These two systems are also used to monitor any other objects of interest to Soviet intelligence personnel.

The RORSAT is used for military observation of Western naval movements. RORSAT (Radar Ocean Reconnaissance Satellite) is equipped with a radar system which is powered by a small nuclear reactor fueled by Uranium-235. The satellite operates in low earth orbit (about 150 miles). After serving its operational mission (usually from several weeks to months), the satellite jettisons its nuclear reactor—which is pushed into a very high orbit so that the radioactive material may decay. On two occasions nuclear reactors fell into the atmosphere, contaminating two areas on earth: in northwest Canada in 1978 and the southern Indian Ocean in 1983. Because of its ability to accurately track ships (and quite possibly submarines), RORSAT is a real concern for defense planners.

EORSAT is an electronic intelligence reconnaissance satellite system. Generally operating at an altitude of about 280 miles, these satellites are often used in tandem to monitor American communications and radar emissions from naval movements.

The MOLNIYA (Russian for 'lightning') satellite incorporates a 12 hour semisynchronous orbital path and is used

for missile warning. They keep watch for rocket launches anywhere in the world, particularly from North America. In spite of the obvious military nature of these satellites, the Russians have never officially acknowledged their purpose. In the official published data on orbiting satellites they are simply scientific research vehicles.

The over-the-horizon radar of the Russian ballistic missile defense system consists of 11 large ballistic missile early warning radars at six locations on the periphery of the Soviet Union. Designated HEN HOUSE radars by US defense planners, these radars can distinguish the size of an attack, confirm the warning from the satellite system and provide target tracking data in support of anti-ballistic missile defense forces.

The third operational layer of the Soviet system for detection and tracking of a ballistic missile attack is the new large phased-array radars now under construction. This new network of six radars can track ballistic missiles with greater accuracy than the existing system. Five of these radars supplement the coverage of the existing system. The sixth radar, which is now under construction at Krasnoyarsk, Siberia completes the Soviet early radar coverage. The combined network of six large phased-array radars will form an arc of coverage from the Kola Peninsula in the northwest Soviet Union, around Siberia to the Caucasus in the southwest.

In signing the 1972 ABM Treaty both the United States and the Soviet Union recognized the need for ballistic missile early warning radars. With this in mind, the construction of

Conceptual Illustrations shown *above, upper right* and *lower right,* in order: The Soviet HEN HOUSE Ballistic Missile Early Warning System; Soviet DOG HOUSE radar; and a Large, Phased-Array Ballistic Missile Detection and Tracking Radar installation at Krasnoyarsk.

the new large phased-array radars by the Soviets is not a violation of the accords. Indeed, the United States is also constructing new ballistic missile early warning radars, which are located on the periphery of our territory and oriented outward (in other words, away from the continental United States). The US and Soviets also recognized that ballistic early warning radars can detect and track warheads at great distances, and as a result, have a significant anti-ballistic missile potential. This sort of capability would play an important role in a national ABM defense, which is what the 1972 Treaty was designed to prevent. This is why the treaty signatories agreed that new ballistic missile early warning radars would only be located on the periphery of each nation and oriented outward. In this way the legitimate need for early warning against attack could be satisfied, while minimizing the opportunity for the construction of an effective nationwide battle management network.

In 1983 an American reconnaissance satellite first spotted the now-famous giant radar facility near Abalakono in the Krasnoyarsk region of Central Siberia deep inside the Soviet Union. According to US analysts, the new large phased-array radar being built at Krasnoyarsk violates the 1972 ABM Treaty. Tall as a 50-story building and as large as two football fields, the radar is most likely designed for ballistic

missile detection and tracking, including ballistic early warning (which is not in itself a problem). According to the treaty specifics, such radar must either be within a 90 mile radius of the national capital (Moscow) or located on the periphery of the nation and oriented outward. The radar under construction is about 2200 miles from Moscow and 450 miles from the nearest border at Mongolia. Further—and perhaps most alarming to the US analysts—the radar is oriented not outwards towards the Mongolian border, but towards the northeast across 2400 miles of Soviet territory. The Soviet Union claims that this particular radar is designed for space tracking—not ballistic missile early warning—and therefore does not come under the jurisdiction of the ABM Treaty. However, (according to US analysts) its design is not optimized for a space tracking role. In fact the Krasnoyarsk radar design is essentially identical to that of other radars which, as acknowledged by the Soviets, are for ballistic missile detection and tracking—including ballistic missile early warning.

The ever-growing network of Soviet ABM efforts is of particular concern to the United States. The large phased-array radars take years to construct. Once completed, the Soviet Union could decide to build a nationwide ABM defense and do so rather quickly if they so choose. Apparently the Soviets are developing components of a new ABM system which seems to be designed to allow the construction of individual ABM sites—in a matter of months rather than the years which are now required for more traditional ABM systems. If in fact these components are developed, these activities would also be in technical violation of the ABM treaty prohibition against the development of a mobile landbased ABM system. US analysts estimate that by using such components, the Soviets could undertake rapidly-paced ABM deployments to strengthen the defenses of Moscow and to defend key targets in the western USSR and east of the Urals by the early 1990s.

The Soviet ABM activities are considered ominous by the United States. Taken together, these activities could suggest that the USSR may be preparing an anti-ballistic missile defense of its national territory. Further, before too long the Soviets would be able to announce their decision to withdraw from the ABM Treaty and rapidly expand their defenses.

Of equal concern are the Soviet defense-related activities in space. The Soviet Union inaugurated the space age in October of 1957 when it injected Sputnik I, a 185 pound instrument package, into earth orbit. Less than 30 years later the Soviets were sending packages into space at a rate of about 100 launchings per year, accounting for as much as three-quarters of the world's total launches. Through the years the Soviet space engineers have worked toward three major longterm goals. First, the establishment of a permanent manned space platform for space research. Second, the development of a wide variety of satellites for particular applications such as communications and meteorology, but also for surveillance and tracking. Finally, the development of a significant war fighting capability from space. This includes space-to-atmosphere and space-to-ground as well as space-to-space capabilities.

They would seem to be well on their way to achieving these goals. For more than a dozen years now, the Soviet Union has apparently had an operational anti-satellite system. The Soviet 'killer' satellite is an approximately three ton spacecraft armed with an explosive charge. The satellite is a co-orbital device which is launched into the same orbital plane as that of its target. After the 'killer' satellite gets into close proximity to its target (usually within three hours following launch of the 'killer'), it destroys that target satellite by exploding a conventional warhead.

In addition to the 'killer' satellite, Western military analysts are particularly concerned with the Russian research program of advanced technology for defense against ballistic missiles. Begun in the late 1960s, the Soviet research program covers many of the technologies included in the US Strategic Defense Initiative. However, the effort by the Soviet Union represents a far greater investment in capital, facilities and human resources than the US program. Of particular interest to the United States are the Soviet programs for laser weapons, particle beam weapons, radio frequency weapons, kinetic energy weapons and computer and sensor technology.

The laser research program in the Soviet Union is much larger than similar efforts in the United States. The Russian effort apparently involves over 10,000 scientists and engi-

The parade goes on: Seen on Red Square, in demonstration of the success of the 1917 Revolution, a Soviet SS-8 ICBM (*above left*) heavily trundles among the festivities, as do Soviet SS-11 ICBMs (*above*), seen *here* against the large propaganda backdrop of a Soviet worker freeing the world from its chains with his presumably nuclear hammer. The Soviet 'evangelism' continues.

neers spread over more than a half-dozen major research and development facilities and test ranges. A majority of the research takes place at the Sary Shagan Missile Test Center on the banks of Lake Balkhash in Kazakhstan (which is roughly south of Siberia), where the Soviet Union also conducts traditional ABM research. Shagan Test Center facilities are estimated to include several air defense lasers, a laser that may be capable of damaging some components of satellites in orbit and a laser that could be used in feasibility testing for ballistic missile defense applications. A laser weapons program in the United States which approximated the magnitude of the Soviet Union effort would cost roughly $1 billion per year.

The Soviets are apparently conducting research in three types of gas lasers considered promising for weapons applications. These types are the gas-dynamic laser, the electric discharge laser and the chemical laser. Success in laser research is measured in terms of output power, and Soviet achievements in this area have been impressive. The Soviets have also shown interest in the military potential of visible and very short wavelength lasers. They are investigating eximer, free electron and X-ray lasers, and have been developing argonion lasers for more than ten years.

A major consideration for lasers, as well as other directed-energy weapons, is power. The Soviets appear generally capable of supplying the prime power, energy storage and auxiliary components needed for their advanced technology weaponry. They have developed a rocket-driven magneto-hydrodynamic generator which produces over 15 megawatts of electrical power. This particular type of power source is

unique to the Soviet Union—there is no counterpart as powerful in the West. The Soviets may also have the capability to develop the optical systems necessary for laser weaponry. These optical systems would be used to track and attack targets. This estimate of capability is based on the Soviets' successful production of a four foot segmented mirror for an astrophysical telescope in 1978. The Soviet Union claimed that this mirror was to be a prototype for an 82.5 foot segmented mirror which would be constructed in the future. A large mirror such as this is considered necessary for a groundbased laser weapon.

US analysts believe that in some areas, the Soviet Union has now progressed beyond the technology research phase. The Soviets have groundbased lasers which could be used to interfere with US satellites. In addition, by the late 1980s the Russians could have prototypes for groundbased lasers to be used for defense against ballistic missiles. Further, the Soviets could begin testing components for a large scale groundbased laser deployment system in the early 1990s. There is much for the Russians to overcome, however. The difficulties which will likely be encountered in fielding an operational system will require more development effort. With this in mind, an operational groundbased laser for defense of the USSR against ballistic missiles could probably not be deployed until the late 1990s—or perhaps not until after the year 2000.

Above right: This directed-energy research and development site at the USSR's Sary Shagan facility could well provide ASAT capability in the future. An artist's conception of a future Soviet directed-energy weapon (*below*) indicates the large energy-supply system it would need.

If technology developments prove successful, the USSR could deploy operational spacebased anti-satellite lasers sometime in the 1990s, and would possibly be able to deploy spacebased laser systems against ballistic missiles after the year 2000.

Particle beam weapons are another phase of Soviet directed energy research. A particle beam is a stream of atoms or subatomic particles (electrons, protons, or neutrons) which are accelerated to nearly the speed of light. A particle beam weapon, then, relies on the technology of particle accelerators to emit beams of either charged (protons and electrons) or neutral (neutrons) particles. Such a beam could theoretically destroy a target by several means. The USSR has been involved in research to explore the feasibility of spacebased particle beam weapons since the late 1960s. US military analysts estimate that they may be able to test a prototype particle beam weapon by the 1990s. This prototype would be intended to disrupt the electronics of satellites; however, there is the possibility of a follow-on weapon designed actually to destroy satellites. At this point in their research, a weapon which has the capability to destroy missile boosters or warheads will probably require several additional years of research and development.

At this point in time, it appears that particle beam weapons must be spacebased. It is not clear whether ground-based charged particle beam weapons are feasible; in other words, will the beam propagate in the atmosphere? Up to now, stable propagation of particle beams in the atmosphere has never been demonstrated. This is not the case *above* the atmosphere, however. A spacebased neutral particle beam would not be affected by atmospheric conditions—or for that matter, by the magnetic field of earth.

Soviet efforts in particle beam research are impressive. They have made considerable strides in the areas of ion sources and radio frequency quadruple accelerators for particle beams. As a matter of fact, much of the American understanding as to how particle beams could be made into practical defensive weaponry is based on Soviet research conducted in the late 1960s and early 1970s.

One final note regarding Soviet research on directed-energy weaponry: The Soviet Union has conducted research in the use of strong radio frequency signals which have the potential to interfere with—or perhaps destroy—critical electronic components in ballistic missile warheads. It is possible that in the 1990s, the Soviets could test a ground-based radio frequency weapon with the capability of damaging satellites.

The Soviet Union also has a variety of ongoing research programs in the area of kinetic energy weapons. Such weapons destroy targets through the use of nonexplosive projectiles moving at very high speeds. The projectiles may include homing sensors and onboard rockets to improve accuracy or they may follow a present trajectory, much like a shell launched from a gun or cannon. The projectile could be launched from a rocket, a conventional gun or a rail gun. Rail guns utilize a system of electromagnets to launch projectiles. These guns would have very high muzzle velocities, thereby reducing the lead angle required to shoot down fast-moving objects. If fired in the atmosphere, this fast muzzle velocity would reduce windage effects and flatten trajectories.

In the 1960s, the Soviet Union developed an experimental gun that could shoot streams of particles of heavy metals such as tungsten or molybdenum, at speeds of nearly 15 miles per second in air and something over 36 miles per second in a vacuum.

It is not likely that spacebased kinetic energy weapons for defense against ballistic missiles could be developed until the mid-1990s or, perhaps even later. It is possible however, that in the near future the USSR could deploy a short-range, spacebased system for satellite or space station defense. It is also possible that the Soviets could use kinetic energy weaponry for close-in attack by a maneuvering satellite. The Soviet Union's capabilities in guidance and control systems are now satisfactory for the development of effective space-based kinetic energy weapons systems.

The key to any successful advanced weapons system—whether offensive or defensive; whether space- or ground-based; whether directed-energy or kinetic energy technology—is absolutely dependent upon remote sensor and sophisticated computer technology. At this point sensor and computer technology is much more advanced in the West than in

than in the Soviet Union. As a result the Soviets are devoting considerable resources to improving their capabilities and expertise in these technologies. A significant part of the Soviet effort involves an ever-increasing exploitation of Western technology. This exploitation includes free access information gathering as well as clandestine operations. It is well known that the Soviets have long been engaged in a well-funded effort to purchase US high-technology computers, test and calibration data and remote sensor devices illegally through third parties.

For the past 20 years, assumptions of how nuclear deterrence can best be assured have been based on the basic idea of Mutually Assured Destruction. That is, if each side maintains the ability to retaliate against any attack and impose on an aggressor costs that are out of balance with any potential gains, the threat will prevent attacks. This assumption served as the foundation for the US approach to the Strategic Arms Limitation Talks (SALT).

The Soviet Union remains the principal threat to US security and to that of its allies. As part of its wide ranging effort to increase its military capabilities, the Soviet Union's improvement of its military force has threatened the survivability of the forces deployed by the US and its allies (which

are aimed at deterring aggression). This missile force also threatens many critical fixed installations in the United States and in allied territories. At the same time, the Soviet efforts to develop and improve active defense systems provide a steadily increasing capability to counter the retaliatory forces of the United States and its allies.

For 20 years the United States has relied on what is known as the 'Strategic Nuclear Triad' as a means of discouraging the Soviet Union from an attack on the territory of the US or its allies. The elements of the famous triad are Minuteman missiles on the land, B-52 bombers in the air and submarine-carried Poseidon and Trident missiles in the sea. Many military analysts believe that two of the three legs of the triad are at best a limited deterrence threat to a potential Soviet aggressive force.

The land leg of the triad, the Minuteman missile system, was originally deployed in the late 1960s and early 1970s as the retaliatory nuclear force of the United States. When the system was originally designed, the Soviet offensive missiles were inaccurate. As a result, the Minuteman launchers (which were distributed around the country) were not particularly threatened by a potential attack. Since that time however, the accuracy of Soviet missiles has improved con-

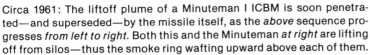

Circa 1961: The liftoff plume of a Minuteman I ICBM is soon penetra-
ted—and superseded—by the missile itself, as the *above* sequence pro-
gresses *from left to right.* Both this and the Minuteman *at right* are lifting
off from silos—thus the smoke ring wafting upward above each of them.

siderably. Indeed the accuracy has improved to the point that
the majority of Minuteman silos could well be destroyed by a
Soviet first strike. The new MX is half the size of the SS-18
and designed to bolster the US retaliatory force.

The second weak link in the American strategic triad is the
aging B-52 bomber. The B-52 fleet is in actuality a force of
antiquated aircraft which have an average age of about 25
years. Designed in a time of less sophisticated radar, B-52s
today have lots of sharp angles and 'hot' spots in their con-
tours which strongly reflect today's radar waves. Further increasing vulnerability is the flight envelope of the B-52.
These old bombers fly at high altitude on their bombing
runs—which makes them easy targets for Soviet radar even
at long distances. Because of their radar vulnerability, it is
not likely that these bombers would be able to penetrate the
air defense system in the event of the need of a retaliatory attack. This is, of course, in the event that the bombers get in
the air at all. Military planners estimate that, since only 30
percent of all B-52s are normally on alert at any one time, it is

Left: Ground crews study a cruise missile pod under the wing of a B-52G. *Below:* On board a B-52, the offensive weapons operator carefully attends his instruments. *Above:* Crewmembers rush toward their B-52 during a 'scramble alert.' *Overleaf:* The B-1B bomber.

likely that the remaining bombers would be destroyed on the ground at the outset of a surprise attack.

The United States equipped the B-52 fleet with air-launched cruise missiles in an attempt to offset some of the major vulnerabilities of the aircraft. The cruise missile is a pilotless jet aircraft equipped with internal navigation capabilities. The cruise missile navigates with radar—it checks the radar return signals against a terrain map stored in an onboard computer. Although cruise missiles do not have intercontinental range, they can be carried to country borders by the B-52 and launched from the air. Effective in concept, the current version of the cruise missile can be shot down by the Soviet Union's SA-10 surface-to-air missiles. It can also be

shot down by the Soviet Foxhound fighter aircraft which is capable of a maximum speed of about 1600 miles per hour and is equipped with 'look down' radar and a 'shoot down' capability.

It is hoped that the new B1-B bomber will restore some of the effectiveness of the air leg of the United States strategic triad. The B1-B has been designed to be significantly less 'eye catching' to Soviet radar than its older cousin, the B-52. It is designed to fly at close to treetop level at nearly the speed of sound enroute to its target, which makes it doubly hard to detect on radar. Congress has approved 100 B1-Bs, and they are expected to be in service by 1987.

The third leg of the US triad is the submarine. It is on this leg that the strategic triad stands—as the United States' fleet of nuclear-powered submarines are currently the only serious deterrent which must be considered by Soviet planners. The newest models (the Trident submarines) have exceptionally quiet engines and an overall shape which is very difficult to pick up on radar. The United States submarine force consists of 36 missile-carrying submarines. The newer vessels have a very long range that gives them a huge expanse of ocean in which to hide and launch their missiles.

The Soviet Union would seem to be on a steady program of improvement of its countermeasure forces in order to fur-

Previous to its 18 October 1984 maiden flight, the first B-1B long range bomber *(below)* undergoes a systems test at Rockwell International's Palmdale facility. SSBN 727 USS *Michigan (left)* can launch 24 Trident C-4 SLBMs, each carrying eight warheads.

ther hinder the strategic triad of the United States. These countermeasures, both offensive and defensive, have caused great alarm on the part of American leaders.

Americans have been hearing for years now that the Soviet system would 'bury' ours. More importantly, we have also heard but perhaps not listened to the Soviets telling us that the struggle to convert us would continue, no matter what the circumstance. No doubt there is a certain amount of rhetoric in this; however, to the Russian leaders this is an ideological issue which must continue even in periods of peaceful coexistence. Following the tumultuous McCarthy years of 'the Communist scare,' presidential administrations tended to downplay the ever-growing Russian threat. John F Kennedy had campaigned for the presidency with a strong warning about the ever-smaller gap in the relative strengths of the United States and the Soviet Union. For the most part, subsequent presidents tended to focus on specific categories of difference with the Soviets and not to look (at least public-ly) at the power struggle between the United States and the Soviet Union.

President Reagan took a different tack however. Early on in his administration—indeed even during his campaign—President Reagan announced that the United States was no longer the world's largest nor strongest military power. As a matter of fact, the US was militarily inferior to the Soviet Union. Mr Reagan specifically blamed our reliance on arms control for causing us to be second to Russia. The admini-stration believed that the United States, in its quest for disar-

Counterclockwise from top, above: The sequential photos on *these pages* demonstrates the kill capability of the McDonnell-Douglas Tomahawk cruise missile, which besides having conventional explosives capability (shown *here),* also can 'boost' a nuclear warhead.

mament, had given up military options and alternatives—which it should have protected. Worse, the United States had exacerbated the problem by allowing the Soviet Union to keep and build on all of their options.

Because the administration had seen the deterioration of the strategic triad, a policy of military buildup was in order to re-establish the overall military and technological superiority of the United States over the Soviet Union. With the sometimes reluctant support of Congress, it was clear by late 1980 that the United States would be back in the arms race. Further, the administration wanted to suspend bilateral arms control negotiations and focus on a unilateral US rearmament until such time as equality was re-established. Actually the Reagan Administration looked to surpass the Soviets and obtain a 'margin of safety' before returning to the bargaining table.

And so in response to the long-term pattern of Soviet offensive improvements, the leaders of the United States felt compelled to pursue complementary actions. These actions were designed both to maintain US security and stability in the near term and to insure stability in the future. Three areas were targeted for action: First—modernize US offensive nuclear retaliatory forces; second—continue with a strong commitment to arms control; finally—develop, through expanded research and development in advanced technologies, effective defense systems (both ground- and spacebased), which offer both stability and hopefully, mutual benefits for the US and USSR.

In 1981 the United States began a modernization program for its offensive nuclear weapons fleet. This program was designed to preserve a stable deterrence and at the same time, to provide the incentives required to get the Soviet Union to negotiate with the United States on significantly reducing the nuclear arsenals of both sides. Here was the sticking point in the negotiations: The United States wanted to negotiate arms reductions for the Soviets while at the same time pursuing an arms buildup at home. Whether the Soviet Union had a strategic advantage or not, it was not likely that the Soviets would consider reductions in the face of buildup in America. Compounding the situation, NATO, the British and the French also embarked on programs to modernize their strategic nuclear retaliatory forces.

Even while these offensive modernization programs were underway, the United States had a near-term objective to reduce significantly worldwide nuclear arms. According to the United States the goals for arms control talks were significant reductions—the deeper the reduction, the better the agreement relative to United States interests; and the more the reduction in Soviet nuclear weapons, the better the stability of the peace between the Soviet Union and the United States. Arms limitation discussions will be aimed at achieving this objective through negotiated limitation agreements that are both equitable and verifiable. The United States took a hard line on cutbacks, insisting on drastic reductions in the most modern and potent Soviet weapons—many of which were already deployed. At the same time, the United States would not consider reductions in comparable existing American forces.

As could be expected, the relationship between the Soviets and Americans was very quickly at a tense standoff—each side pointing a finger at the other and claiming foul play; each side showing how the other was after a 'first strike' advantage; and each side probably looking for that very advantage. Over the years, arms control talks between the US and

Leonid Brezhnev (*above*) led the Soviets to lighten their economic and ideological competition with the US in the 1970s, working instead on an unprecedented Soviet arms buildup. Wait till you see the bill: an LGM-118 'MX' missile blasts off (*right*) at Vandenberg AFB.

USSR had weathered all sorts of threats and walkouts. By the early years of this decade however, the strain had begun to show. In the view of the Soviets, the United States had deliberately begun a time of confrontation which was not in the spirit of detente. Since that was the case, the Soviets would also give up on detente—and arms control would be a thing of the past.

What followed was a period of 'saber rattling' in the form of weapons testing on both sides. Both sides looked to find a way to force the other back to the bargaining table. The United States took a very aggressive posture in 1983 with the announcing of the Strategic Defense Initiative. The decision to make this announcement was probably precipitated by the discovery of the Krasnoyarsk radar facility—coupled with something more ominous. Early on in 1983, the Soviet Union test-fired a series of SS-20 missiles on a trajectory toward the United States. Although these missiles were destroyed by the Soviets and called test vehicles, the United States leadership took the launches to be warning messages. Since the US had already embarked on a very large rearmament program, the obvious next step was for defense.

Defensive systems were considered necessary to eliminate the current (or potential) out-of-balance condition between the USSR and the United States. The Strategic Defense In-

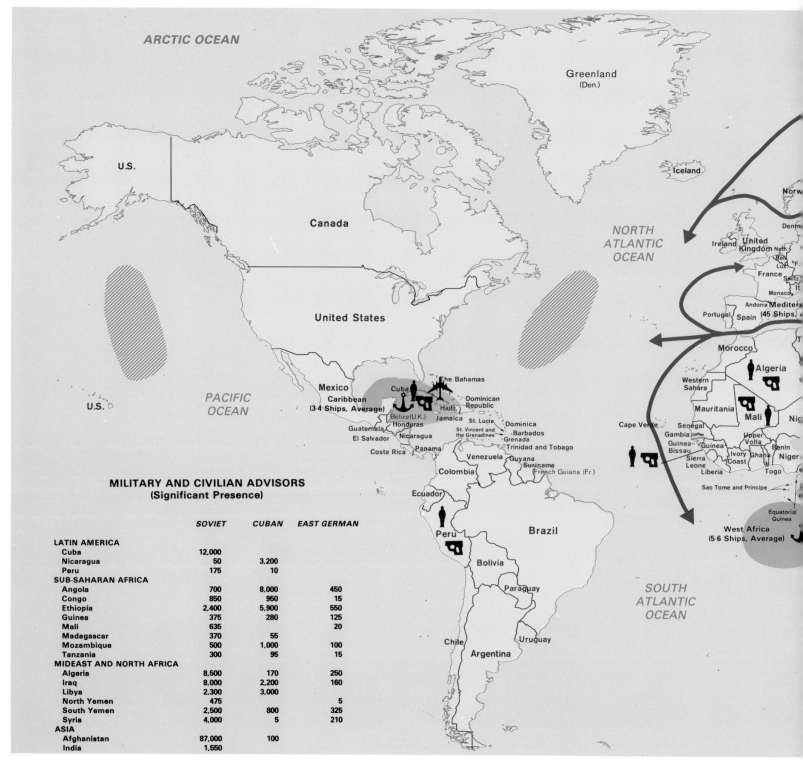

ARCTIC OCEAN

Greenland (Den.)

U.S.

Canada

NORTH ATLANTIC OCEAN

Iceland

United States

PACIFIC OCEAN

U.S.

Mexico
Caribbean
(3-4 Ships, Average)

The Bahamas
Cuba
Haiti
Dominican Republic
Belize (U.K.)
Jamaica
St. Lucia
Dominica
Honduras
Guatemala
El Salvador
Nicaragua
Costa Rica
Panama
St. Vincent and the Grenadines
Barbados
Grenada
Trinidad and Tobago
Venezuela
Guyana
Suriname
French Guiana (Fr.)
Colombia
Ecuador
Peru
Brazil
Bolivia
Paraguay
Chile
Uruguay
Argentina

Ireland
United Kingdom
Neth.
Denm.
Norw.
Bel.
Lux.
France
Switz.
Monaco
Andorra
Portugal
Spain
(45 Ships)
Mediter.
Morocco
Algeria
Western Sahara
Mauritania
Mali
Niger
Cape Verde
Senegal
Gambia
Guinea-Bissau
Guinea
Sierra Leone
Liberia
Ivory Coast
Upper Volta
Ghana
Togo
Benin
Sao Tome and Principe
Equatorial Guinea
West Africa
(5-6 Ships, Average)

SOUTH ATLANTIC OCEAN

MILITARY AND CIVILIAN ADVISORS
(Significant Presence)

	SOVIET	CUBAN	EAST GERMAN
LATIN AMERICA			
Cuba	12,000		
Nicaragua	50	3,200	
Peru	175	10	
SUB-SAHARAN AFRICA			
Angola	700	8,000	450
Congo	850	950	15
Ethiopia	2,400	5,900	550
Guinea	375	280	125
Mali	635		20
Madagascar	370	55	
Mozambique	500	1,000	100
Tanzania	300	95	15
MIDEAST AND NORTH AFRICA			
Algeria	8,500	170	250
Iraq	8,000	2,200	160
Libya	2,300	3,000	
North Yemen	475		5
South Yemen	2,500	800	325
Syria	4,000	5	210
ASIA			
Afghanistan	87,000	100	
India	1,550		

itiative was therefore specifically aimed at bringing the strategic environment back into balance. Further, the Strategic Defense Initiative was intended to respond directly to the extensive Soviet anti-ballistic missile effort. Hopefully, the Strategic Defense Initiative could also provide a powerful deterrent to any potential Soviet decision to withdraw from the 1972 ABM treaty and rapidly expand its antiballistic missile capability. Finally, remembering the United States' commitment to arms control, it was hoped that the Strategic Defense Initiative would offer compelling incentives for the Soviet Union to join in serious negotiations with the specific intent to limit offensive weaponry and stabilize the world environment.

Before we go on to explore more about the Strategic Defense Initiative, it is important that we consider first the situation in which the Russians find themselves. The original

doctrine of communism was not unlike the scientific principle of critical mass. It was postulated that when people revolted, a chain reaction would have begun and the people all over the world would follow suit. At first, it was considered just a matter of time before the world would follow the lead of the Russian people. Later, it became clear that the world would not follow and that all the revolution had accomplished was the formation of another state (albeit a very large one).

After World War II, when Stalin dominated the newly acquired territories, it seemed possible that the working classes in the more democratic West would finally choose to revolt. For at least a decade, Soviet-financed unions throughout Europe threatened to attract a majority of workers and bring about radical change. Further, the Communist Party, directly controlled from Moscow, attracted a large following of

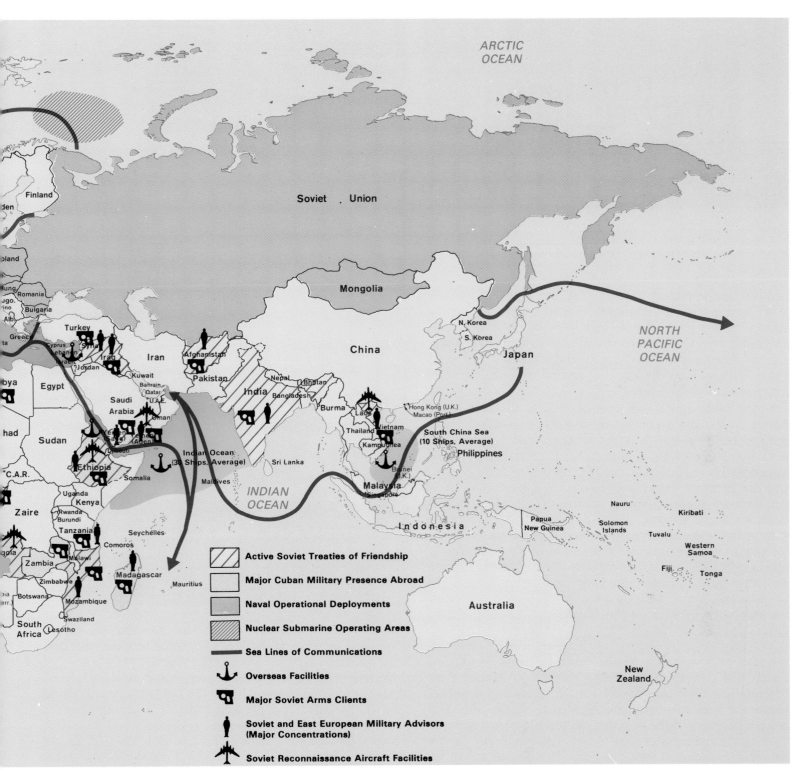

ARCTIC
OCEAN

Soviet · Union

Mongolia

China

N. Korea

S. Korea

Japan

NORTH
PACIFIC
OCEAN

Finland

Turkey

Iran

Afghanistan

Pakistan

Nepal

Bhutan

India

Bangladesh

Burma

Laos

Hong Kong (U.K.)

Macao (Port.)

Thailand

Vietnam

Kampuchea

South China Sea
(10 Ships, Average)

Philippines

Indian Ocean
(30 Ships, Average)

Sri Lanka

INDIAN
OCEAN

Brunei
(U.K.)

Malaysia
Singapore

Indonesia

Nauru

Kiribati

Papua
New Guinea

Solomon
Islands

Tuvalu

Western
Samoa

Fiji

Tonga

Australia

Cyprus

Lebanon

Israel

Syria

Iraq

Jordan

Kuwait

Bahrain

Qatar

U.A.E.

Saudi
Arabia

Oman

Egypt

Sudan

Ethiopia

Somalia

Maldives

Seychelles

Comoros

Madagascar

Mauritius

C.A.R.

Uganda

Kenya

Rwanda

Burundi

Tanzania

Zaire

Zambia

Malawi

Zimbabwe

Mozambique

Botswana

Swaziland

South
Africa

Lesotho

New
Zealand

Active Soviet Treaties of Friendship

Major Cuban Military Presence Abroad

Naval Operational Deployments

Nuclear Submarine Operating Areas

Sea Lines of Communications

⚓ **Overseas Facilities**

Major Soviet Arms Clients

**Soviet and East European Military Advisors
(Major Concentrations)**

Soviet Reconnaissance Aircraft Facilities

trade union leaders and members and intellectual leaders throughout the world.

Somehow, over the years there has been a noticeable decline in the appeal of the communist ideology. Perhaps this was a result of the success of nations which chose to leave the central Moscow fold. China went its own way, Poland has been fiercely independent and Czechoslovakia had to be literally crushed into submission. This decline in the appeal of communism probably led to the shift of Soviet efforts away from broad social and political action (although this has not been eliminated entirely) to the buildup of power in the world through military might. Early on, the Russian leadership was seemingly aware of an elemental fact of world psychology—which is that as the relative power of a nation increases, the perception of that nation's sphere of influence also increases. In other words, a nation with exceptional

Above: This map and its accompanying symbols graphically portray Soviet military power world-wide as of 1982. Biased as such political maps generally are, one may note that one of the regions shown as having 'Active Soviet Treaties of Friendship' is Afghanistan.

military strength will be allowed to take advantage of that strength, because nations of lesser strength do not care to risk war. This principle was clearly demonstrated in the years before World War II as nations 'appeased' Hitler by allowing Germany to gobble up vast amounts of Europe.

In the days before nuclear weapons, this psychology worked exceptionally well. Although the principle remains the same today, the stakes have changed considerably. Now, power is a function of weapons which cannot be used and the balance is forever shifting to the side with more power. In the seesaw power struggle with the United States (and in light of the decline of the appeal of communism), the Soviets took a

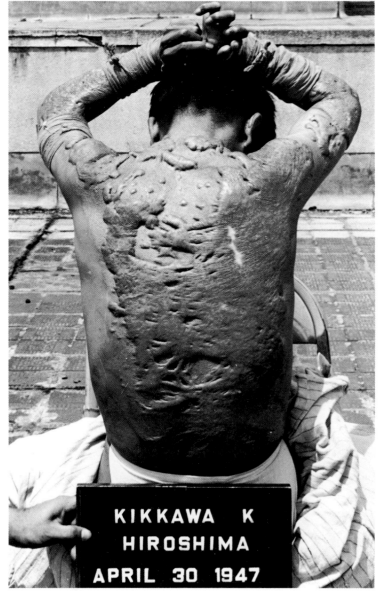

The devastation of Hiroshima after the 'Little Boy' detonation: As viewed by Doctor Nagai (*far right*), himself a radiation victim; a radiation burns victim *at immediate right;* its slight blast resistance enabled this building (*above*) to 'survive' a half mile from ground zero.

two-pronged approach to furthering their course. The first, as we have noted, is a massive, focused program of armament. The cost never seems to high or the quantity too much; the goal is world power through military strength. The other aspect of their approach is directed at discrediting the United States. The goal is to find ways to separate the United States from its allies and friends.

Today, although it has friends around the world, the Soviet Union is surrounded by the other so-called 'super powers' of the world. It is known that besides Russia and America, three other countries have arsenals of nuclear weapons. These countries are the United Kingdom, France, and the People's Republic of China. It is more than likely that the nuclear arms of these countries are aimed squarely at the heart of the Soviet Union. Although when compared to Russian (or even American) strength, these weapons are technically weak, no nuclear weapon can be considered insignificant. Ironically, it is the very strength of the Soviet Union which no doubt causes these countries directly to face the Soviets. The Soviets have to some extent caused a loose cooperation of otherwise not-too-friendly (or at least argumentative) neighbors.

There is a vicious cycle at work today. The Soviets, surrounded by a seemingly hostile world (of super powers, at least), feel compelled to protect themselves against these potential enemies. In turn, the United States and the other remaining super powers feel threatened by the huge and growing strength of the Russians and feel compelled to develop weapons to counter that threat. Each side talks about balancing power, but each side wants to maintain an advantage.

Depending upon how weapons and forces are counted, the might of the Russians is equal to that of the Americans. The most frightening element of our existence today is the realization that the struggle of our two countries (over ideology, interests, territory) is likely to continue well into the future. Since there are nuclear-armed intercontinental ballistic missiles situated all over the world, there is a chance that someday the proverbial 'button' may·be pushed, and the doomsday cycle could begin.

The need for a defense against missiles today is the realization that an 'accident' by one side or another could present the chilling prospect of escalation to an exchange which would end the world as we know it. But at the same time we must recognize the potential danger of SDI. As the components of the Strategic Defense Initiative are assembled, we must consider how they are viewed by the leaders of the Soviet Union. If you were Russian and saw that the United States was developing the capability to undermine your strategic alternatives, what would your reaction be?

As technology improved our lives, it also increased the efficiency of killing in war. During the last two years of World War II, 24 million people were killed. Few died of natural causes; the people died from various devices which have been invented to wipe out enemies. This terrible price of 24 million people was accepted as the cost of war—and everyone knew that war was 'inevitable.'

By 1945 the new technology was nuclear, and we had unwittingly 'upped the stakes' of war. Interestingly, the scientists who invented the first atomic weapon were largely unaware of the radiation effects of an atomic blast. They realized that there would be radiation, but they had not imagined that the deadly effects would last after the explosion. In fact, when the Manhattan Project scientists heard of mysterious deaths well after the atomic detonation over Hiroshima, they dismissed the reports as propaganda. They believed that the nuclear bomb was simply a big bang and not a deadly poison as well.

Even after conclusive proof that nuclear weapons were deadly for more reasons than just the explosion, these devices were still built and stockpiled. In war, when you have a weapon you use it—especially if the other side does not have a similar weapon. President Eisenhower threatened to

use nuclear power against North Korea, as well as in Eastern Europe against the Russians. Whether the Soviet Union has a strategic advantage or not, it is likely that NATO, the British and the French will moderize their strategic nuclear forces.

War is so ingrained in our behavior that even now, when our technology has given us a way to destroy everything on Earth, we continue to arm ourselves. Given this willingness to arm, we must also have some sort of defense against the eventual battle. The people of ancient civilizations built fortresses to protect themselves from eventual attack. The for-

tress concept lasted until humans had the capability to use nuclear weapons. With the advent of intercontinental ballistic missiles, the science of defense planning had to catch up with offensive capability. The Strategic Defense Initiative has provided (in concept at least) the possibility of developing a sophisticated multitiered defense system. Such a system could defend against enemy ballisitic missiles in all phases of their flight, rather than only in the terminal phase—where decoys and multiple independent reentry vehicles (MIRVs) constitute a large number of objects with which a defense must cope.

THE STRATEGIC DEFENSE INITIATIVE—AN OVERVIEW

Following the president's speech announcing the Strategic Defense Initiative, two study efforts were established. The first was the Future Strategic Strategy Study. This effort was to determine the implicatons for United States defense policy, strategy and arms control. The study was conducted by two teams of experts; one led by Franklin C Miller and another by Fred S Hoffman. The second study effort was the Defensive Technology Study, commonly referred to as the Fletcher Study after its leader Dr James Fletcher. This effort studied the technologies and systems for ballistic missile defense. These two studies form the basis for the Strategic Defense Initiative concept, both as the focus for research as well as for determining potential strategic consequences. Because of this, these two efforts merit some consideration.

Based on the analyses of the Future Strategic Strategy Study, it was possible that an effective, fully deployed US ballistic missile defense could significantly reduce the military utility of any possible preemptive attack by the Soviet Union. This could in turn potentially increase both deterrence and strategic stability. A ballistic missile defense such as this could only remain effective however if the Soviet

At left: The first color photo of an atomic explosion, taken at a distance of 10 miles at the Alamogordo, New Mexico test site in 1946. *Above right:* An artist's conception reveals one Strategic Defense Initiative strategy.

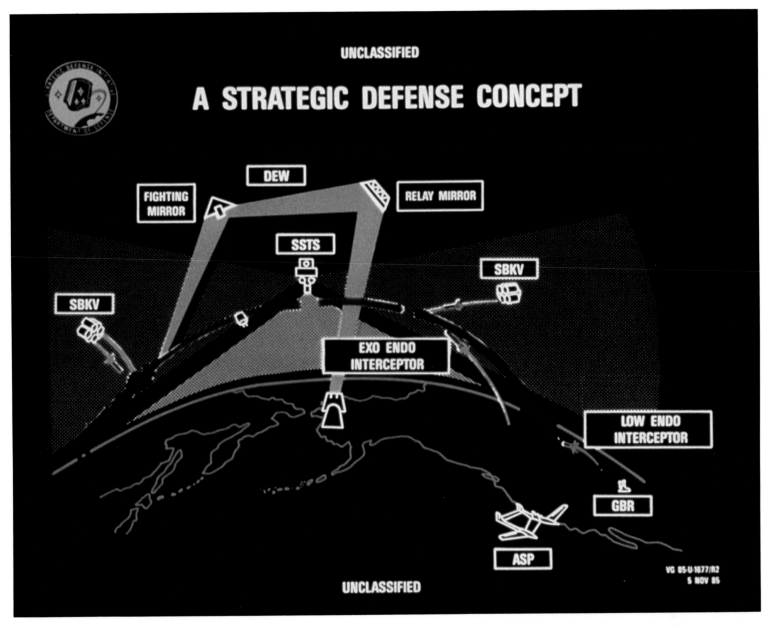

Union could not negate it with countermeasures more cheaply than the United States could maintain the viability of the system.

A basic assumption of the study team was that effective defenses strengthen deterrence by increasing an attacker's uncertainty and undermining an aggressor's confidence in the ability to achieve a predictable, successful outcome. By constraining or perhaps eliminating altogether the effectiveness of both limited and major attack options against key United States military targets, defense systems could significantly reduce the utility of both strategic and limited-theater nuclear forces. This in turn would offer the advantage of lessening the opportunity for nuclear conflict.

The group considered a vigorous research and development effort essential to assess and provide the US with options for future ballistic missile defenses. At the very least, a research program is necessary if only to ensure that in the future the United States will not be faced with a one-sided Soviet deployment of highly effective ballistic missile defenses. If this occurrence did happen, the US would be left with only the weak strategy of a further expansion of our offensive forces.

On the brighter side, if US research efforts on defensive technologies prove successful, the nature of the strategic relationship between the United States and the Soviet Union could, in the US view, be favorably altered. Advanced ballistic missile defenses have the potential for reducing the military value of ballistic missiles and more importantly, lessening their overall role in the strategic balance of these two nations.

The key for our future lies in two study conclusions. First—in reducing the value of ballistic missiles, defensive technologies could substantially increase Soviet incentives to reach agreements calling for the reduction of nuclear arms. It is hoped that the Soviets may become convinced that the American commitment to the deployment of defenses is serious and that the USSR is sure that there are good prospects for eventual success in the development of ballistic missile defenses. Such convincing would then (again hopefully) present opportunities for a safer nuclear relationship between the United States and the Soviet Union.

The second key finding is one of diminished threat. The threat of massive nuclear destruction could be drastically diminished by way of a combined package of air defense, negotiated constraints on all types of offensive nuclear forces and highly effective ballistic missile defenses. Without such a package, the study concludes, we condemn future US presidents and Congresses to remain locked into the present exclusive emphasis on deterrence solely through offensive systems—the MAD approach to peace.

The Defensive Technologies Study (the Fletcher Study) analyzed the technological feasibility of developing an effective defense against ballistic missiles. Six specific areas of defense were considered:

- Surveillance, acquisition and tracking directed-energy weapons
- Conventional weaponry
- Battle management, communications and data processing
- System concepts
- Countermeasures and tactics

The study team identified a long-term technically feasible research and development plan for the United States. Further, the work done by the team forms the core of the research and development efforts of the Strategic Defense Initiative. The Fletcher Study report presented five major conclusions. First, that powerful new technologies are now becoming available. Twenty years ago there were no reliable approaches to the problem of boost-phase intercept (that is, intercepting a missile after it has been launched and while the main rocket engines are still lifting the missile into space). Today, multiple approaches now exist which are based on

The NAVSTAR global positioning satellite (*below*) is a valuable navigation and ocean surveillance tool. *At right, above and below:* US aerial recon photos of Cuba's early 1960s Soviet SS-5 IRBM sites. This and other evidence precipitated the Cuban Missile Crisis.

directed-energy concepts such as particle beams, lasers and kinetic energy destruction mechanisms. Second, 20 years ago missile intercept in midcourse (that is, during spaceflight enroute to the target) was difficult because there were no reliable methods for discrimination between decoys and real warheads. Today—with laser imaging radar, tracking capabilities and accurate direct impact projectiles—there is at least the promise of success with the difficulties of midcourse intercept. Finally, until recently computer hardware and software technology was incapable of handling the information requirements of a defensive system. Today's more powerful computers and advances in artificial intelligence will likely be able to overcome the challenge posed by a multi-tiered defense system.

The second conclusion of the study is that focused research and development efforts in designing a comprehensive ballistic missile defense will require strong central management for coordination and control. This concept of central management would allow a planned approach as well as a focus for reporting. Additionally, with one management structure, projects would be time scheduled based on criticality (as determined by the central management) as well as on funding.

Conclusion three suggested that the most effective defensive systems will have multiple layers or tiers. There are four phases of a typical ballistic trajectory. These are:

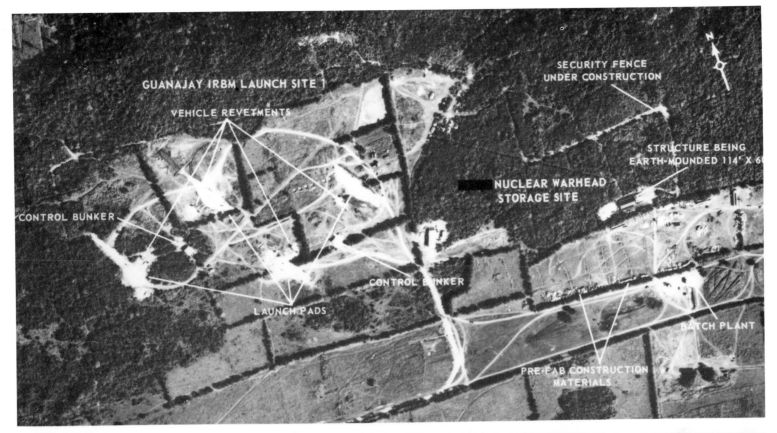

GUANAJAY IRBM LAUNCH SITE 1

SECURITY FENCE
UNDER CONSTRUCTION

VEHICLE REVETMENTS

STRUCTURE BEING
EARTH-MOUNDED 114' X 60'

NUCLEAR WARHEAD
STORAGE SITE

CONTROL BUNKER

CONTROL BUNKER

LAUNCH PADS

BATCH PLANT

PRE-FAB CONSTRUCTION
MATERIALS

5 NOVEMBER 1962

MARIEL PORT

ERECTOR

3 MISSILE TRANSPORTERS

6 MISSILE TRANSPORTERS

MISSILE TRANSPORTERS

IRBM
PROPELLANT TRAILERS

OXIDIZER TRAILERS

- Boost phase—when the first and second stage engines are burning and offering intense, highly specific observable phenomena.
- Postboost phase (also known as 'bus' deployment)—when multiple warheads and penetration aids are released from a postboost vehicle.
- Midcourse phase—when warheads and penetration aids (decoys) travel on ballistic trajectories above Earth's atmosphere.
- Terminal phase—when the warheads and penetration aids re-enter the atmosphere and are affected by atmospheric drag.

A ballistic missile defense system capable of engaging a target all along its flight path must be able to perform some key functions. The system must be able to ward off an attack. This would require global fulltime surveillance of ballistic missile launch areas. The system should have some capability to intercept and destroy boost and postboost vehicles anywhere in their flight trajectory. The system should be able to discriminate between warheads and decoys by filtering out all probable penetration aids. The system must be capable of 'birth-to-death' tracking of all threatening objects. The system must be cost efficient; that is, the cost to the defense for interceptors should be less than the cost to the offense for warheads.

The idea of multilayered defenses is not a new one. However, this concept of a tiered defensive system, with the capabilities noted above, is accepted to be an efficient defense against a high level threat. It is expected that no one tier would be 100 percent effective. For example, a defense sys-

tem composed of three tiers may allow each tier to have a 10 percent leakage (that is, 10 percent of the objects observed in one phase are not intercepted and so move on to the next phase). The overall effectiveness of this system, however, would be about 99.9 percent, and the theoretical overall system leakage of one-tenth of one percent.

The next conclusion presented by the Fletcher study team was that survivability of defense system components is a critical issue. The most likely threats to the components of a defense system are anti-satellite weapons including: ground- or airbased lasers, orbiting anti-satellites, conventional and directed-energy weaponry, space mines, and fragment clouds. Ideally, the defense system should be designed to survive these challenges as well as an all-out attack specifically intended to saturate the system.

The final conclusion of this study team was one relating to progress and time. Demonstrations of new and developing technologies which are critical to an efficient ballistic missile defense system, according to the team, can be performed within the next 10 years. Such demonstrations could include: a spacebased acquisition, tracking and pointing experiments, high power visible light, groundbased laser demonstrations, an airborne optical adjunct demonstration and a high speed endo-atmospheric nonnuclear interceptor missile demonstration.

At right: Lieutenant General James A Abrahamson Jr, the man in charge of SDI. *Below:* A diagram of Responsive Threat Methodology. *Overleaf:* A North American Rockwell artist's view of advanced defense technology—in the sea, on land, in the air and in orbital space—demonstrates an intricate systems interdependence.

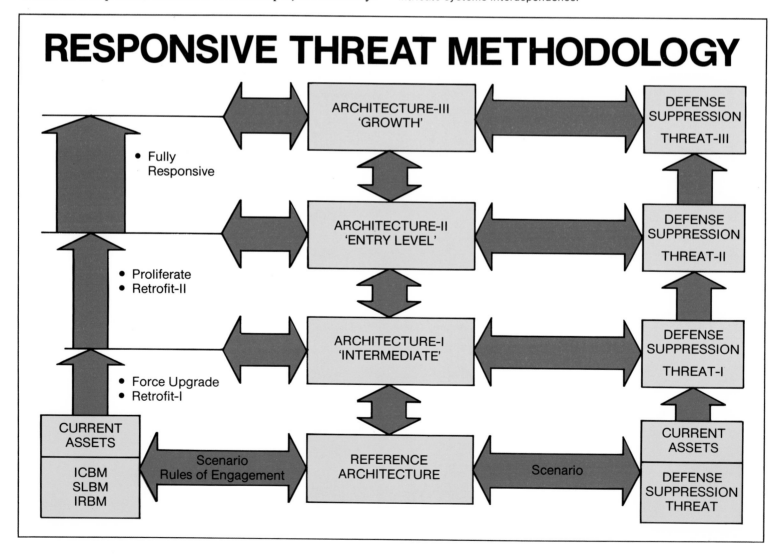

The embodiment of these two comprehensive studies was the Strategic Defense Initiative Organization itself. When the Strategic Defense Initiative was established as a research program, the Strategic Defense Initiative Organization (SDIO) was formed as the defense agency to manage the Department of Defense efforts. The Director of the SDIO reports directly to the Secretary of Defense and is supported by a staff of 100 military and civilian personnel. The staff now consists of both technical and administrative offices which address ongoing scientific research, broad policy issues in conjunction with the Under Secretary of Defense for Policy and, of course, the management of the people and resources of the huge research and development project. The diverse array of technology under consideration necessitates that the director of the Strategic Defense Initiative Organization coordinate

and guide the efforts of various participating and interested organizations. A few of these many organizations are: the Army Strategic Defense Command, the US Air Force, the Defense Nuclear Agency, the Department of Energy and various national laboratories and numerous civilian contractors. In addition, the director of the SDIO must also pay attention to non SDI research activities. In many cases there are non SDI programs which are conducting SDI-related research. This requires close coordination between research entities. Scientific breakthroughs in non SDI research could very well assist SDI efforts. The Defense Advanced Research Project Agency (DARPA) is working on a strategic computing program, for instance. Another example is the Air Force anti-satellite research effort.

Finally, the director of the SDIO must maintain a close working relationship with the federal government. The Strategic Defense Initiative is an important research and development effort. Because of the worldwide impact of SDI, national policy questions require effective coordination between the Department of Defense, the State Department, and officials of the president's administration.

The defense requirements defined by the two study groups were significant and far reaching with this in mind—the Strategic Defense Initiative Organization exists to conduct a program of vigorous research and technology that could lead to specific strategic defense options that could eliminate the threat posed by intercontinental ballistic missiles. These defense options would, hopefully, satisfy three requirements for peace—first, offer an alternative for deterring aggression; second, attempt to strengthen the strategic stability of the world; and third, increase the security of the United States and its allies. The purpose of the Strategic Defense Initiative, therefore, is to provide the technical knowledge required to support an informed decision of whether or not to

The Sprint short-range, high acceleration missile is shown lifting off *at left* in a 1969 test. *Below:* The US Army's long-range Perimeter Acquisition Radar, the 'eye' of the Safeguard ABM system. *At right:* Minuteman III Mark 12s during a test. *At right, below:* Soviet radar coverage.

develop and deploy a defense of the United States and its allies against the offensive threat of intercontinental ballistic missiles. The desired time frame for decisions regarding both development and deployment of Strategic Defense Initiative technologies is somewhere in the early 1990s.

In addition to providing sufficient information for appropriate decisions regarding development and deployment, the success of the SDI program will also be measured in other more subjective areas. The SDI program should be able to counter and (hopefully) discourage the Soviet Union from continuing the growth of their offensive forces. Further, the Strategic Defense Initiative program, by its very existence, should provide a near-term definite response to the aggressive and advanced anti-ballistic missile research and development effort currently underway in the Soviet Union. It is hoped that the SDI program could act as a powerful deterrent to any potential near-term Soviet decision to expand rapidly to anti-ballistic missile systems beyond that contemplated by the articles and amendments of the 1972 Anti-Ballistic Missile Treaty.

Perhaps the most important goal of the Strategic Defense Initiative is one of world stability. Clearly, the concept of

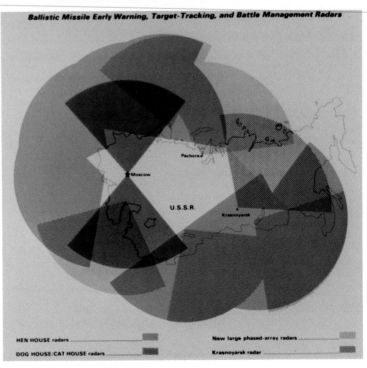

Ballistic Missile Early Warning, Target-Tracking, and Battle Management Radars

HEN HOUSE radars

DOG HOUSE/CAT HOUSE radars

New large phased-array radars

Krasnoyarsk radar

Orbital defense — how do we get satellites in orbit?

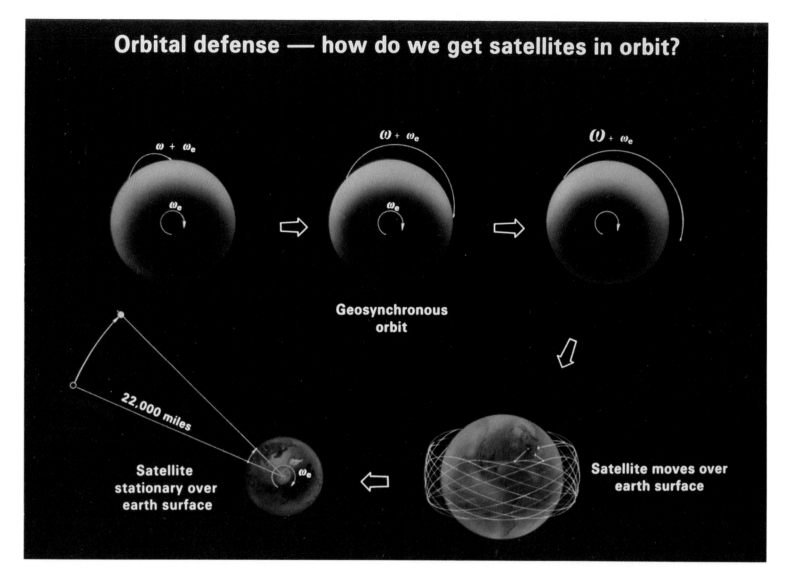

world stability is a vague and subjective term, but by United States standards, SDI offers the possibility of reversing dangerous Russian military trends (both offensive and defensive) by shifting the balance somewhat to a better and (in the US view) more stable basis for deterrence. The Strategic Defense Initiative, even during its research efforts, could also provide new and compelling incentives to the Soviet Union for serious negotiations aimed at reducing existing arsenals of offensive nuclear weapons.

Many ideas can be advanced to describe an ideal defensive system against ballistic missiles. As a research program however, there should be no preconceived notions by the SDIO of what elements an effective defensive system should entail. With this in mind the overall effort of the Strategic Defense Initiative is, for the most part, the examination of a number of different concepts involving a wide range of technologies. At this point no single concept or technology identified can be said to be the best or the most appropriate.

There are however some specific standards which any defensive system recommended by the SDIO would have to meet. These standards apply to all major military systems and may be distilled into three key requirements: first, survivability; second, effectiveness; and third, cost effectiveness.

Advanced defenses must be adequately survivable. In other words, the defenses not only must maintain a satisfactory degree of effectiveness to fulfill their prime function even in the face of determined attacks against those defenses, but also must be able to maintain system stability by discouraging such attacks. To survive, a defensive system must not be an attractive target for defense 'suppression attacks.' If an offensive force is directed against the defense in an attempt to eliminate it, that attacker must be forced to pay a penalty for the aggression. To be effective, this penalty for aggression must be sufficiently high in cost and uncertainty (in achieving the required objectives of the attack) that the offensive move would not be seriously considered. Most importantly, the defensive system must not have an 'Achilles heel'—a specific vulnerability which would defeat the entire system of defense. Survivability for the system does not mean that every element of the defensive system must survive under every circumstance. Rather, the goal of survivability is that the defensive force as a whole, and on an ongoing basis, must be able to achieve its mission despite any degradation in the capability of some of its components. Finally, on a more active basis, whatever the makeup of an actual strategic defense program, system survivability would need to be provided—not only through maneuvering, sensor blinding and shielding materials, but also through such strategic and tactical measures as proliferation, deception and self-defense.

The effectiveness of a major defensive system involves that system's ability to protect against ballistic missile attack. The system defense must be able to destroy enough of an aggressor's attacking forces (in other words, intercontinental ballistic missiles) that the attacker will lack the confidence of being able to achieve an offensive objective. Even in the event that some of an aggressor's force is able to penetrate the defense, an effective defensive system will deny the ag-

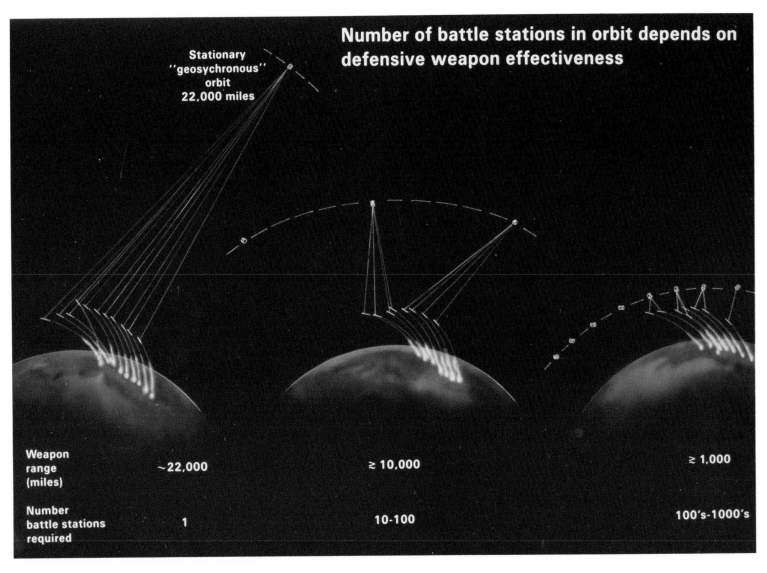

Number of battle stations in orbit depends on defensive weapon effectiveness

Stationary "geosychronous" orbit 22,000 miles

Weapon range (miles)	~22,000	≳ 10,000	≳ 1,000
Number battle stations required	1	10-100	100's-1000's

Above left: This Department of Defense diagram illustrates the placement of satellites in orbit, and their movements once they get there. *Above:* This DOD diagram illustrates the basic working idea of the orbital defense program—'knock them down.'

gressor the ability to destroy a militarily significant portion of the target he wishes to attack. Finally, if a deployed defensive system is to be of lasting value, it must have a design which will allow the evolution of its capabilities. Technology and tactics strategy must be deployed in a fashion which would allow the system to evolve over an extended period as a way to counter any potential responsive threats by an aggressor.

Overall, the SDI program is a search for cost effective defensive options—systems which are able to maintain their capabilities more easily than countermeasures could be taken to defeat them. Cost effectiveness is the expression for an effective system, but it is more than an economic concept. Hopefully it is also a first step toward ongoing, fruitful negotiations and eventually, a less tension-filled peace.

The huge scope of SDI and the relatively short time frame for determining future plans for a strategic defense make the task an extremely complex effort. Without careful control and coordination of the research effort, the project would quickly become simply an extensive list of expensive experiments. Control and co-ordination of the project is dependent upon a five part focus. Success of the project will be based upon the Strategic Defense Initiative Organization's ability to manage five key program elements. Although each element has a different focus, they are all crit-

ically important to the overall effort. These five elements are:

> Option identification
> Technical capability
> Long-range planning
> Short-term planning
> Funding and cost control.

The complexity of the project is clear when one considers that each of these elements are dependent upon the ongoing success of the others and each, in its own way, will affect the success of the overall project.

Since its inception in 1984, the Strategic Defense Initiative Organization has pursued efforts to identify defensive options through System Architecture Studies. The aim of these studies is to profide an initial definition and assessment of several alternatives. Each alternative must be able (theoretically, at least) to detect, identify, discriminate, intercept and destroy ballistic missiles in all phases of flight (that is, boost, postboost, midcourse and terminal phases). Each alternative must have a complete set of technological and functional requirements. Only through the examination of the complete set of requirements can alternatives for sensors, weapons and battle management be mixed for both cost effectiveness and system viability. Option identification also includes a priority list of critical technical issues which must be resolved before a particular defensive strategy may be considered for deployment.

Due to the nature of the task, option identification will be an ongoing effort. The evolution of SDI specific technologies and related issues necessitates the constant review and evolution of defensive system alternatives. The review process must always include an analysis of possible and potential responsive threats (from an aggressor) with which a defensive system will have to cope. Further, once the responsive threats are defined, planners must develop possible event scenarios for use in simulating attacks and evaluating the systems alternatives.

The value of careful and ongoing analysis of options is critical to the success of the Strategic Defense Initiative research. Through the study of possible system alternatives, the SDIO can identify critical problem areas, measure system effectiveness, evolve new concepts and set priorities for investment. As more alternatives are assembled and analyzed, scientists may be able to mix and match components—and in the process, strengthen the overall system.

As the SDI project evolves, the system alternatives identified will become increasingly complex. Ultimately, the systems for final consideration will likely be extremely sophisticated and require computer-simulated battle engagement for accurate evaluation. Not only will the computer simulation assist in analyzing the outcome of a hypothetical battle, it will also provide detailed analysis of how individual components performed under stress. Finally, option identification of defenses will ultimately lead to estimates of cost for development, deployment and operation of each defensive system and component.

Option identification must proceed hand in hand with the careful assessment of technological capability. The Strategic Defense Initiative Organization must conduct a broadly based effort which will expand and accelerate the progress of technology. To be effective, this expansion and acceleration must be conducted in a manner which supports particular defense system architectures. This is accomplished in several ways. First, mature (existing) technologies must be evaluated to offer initial defense system architecture options which are affordable, survivable and effective. Existing technology alternatives will be considered in order to give the United States the option of a deployable defense which could be used against threats between now and early in the next century. The existing technology could also be used as a hedge against the Soviet Union's possibly breaking away from the 1972 ABM Treaty and deploying a defense against the ballistic missiles of the United States.

The SDIO must also consider the long-term viability of existing technologies in light of future defense option needs. Technologies must be able to keep pace with the more advanced defense options which themselves must keep in step with the advancement of the offensive technologies of the early decades of the twenty-first century.

Finally, the SDIO must encourage the research needed to create new technologies to exploit future defense system alternatives. This research will require the inventiveness and innovation of the scientific community as well as the coor-

Below: This diagram emphasizes the critical 'quick kill' factor, which is basic to defense against such fast moving targets as ballistic missiles. *Above right:* This illustration relates the intensity and quickness of focused-energy weapons to their overall defensive effectiveness.

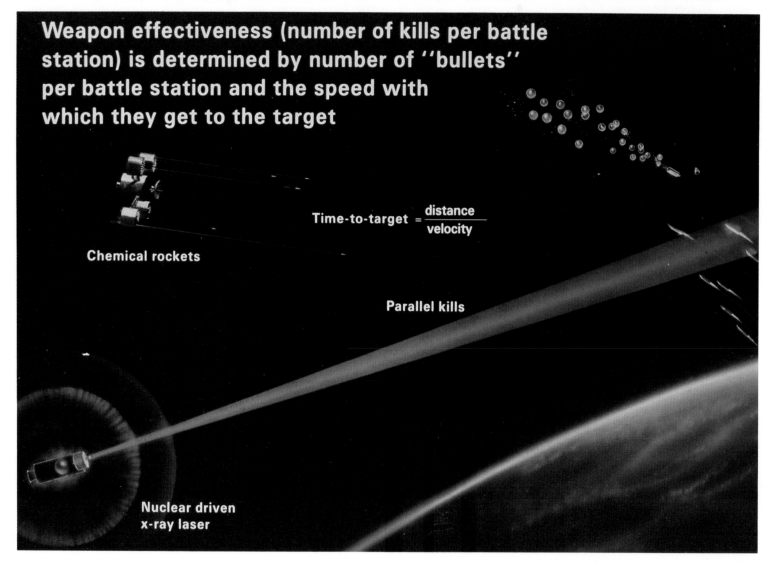

Weapon effectiveness (number of kills per battle station) is determined by number of ''bullets'' per battle station and the speed with which they get to the target

Chemical rockets

$$\text{Time-to-target} = \frac{\text{distance}}{\text{velocity}}$$

Parallel kills

Nuclear driven x-ray laser

Weapon effectiveness (kill rate) is determined by brightness and retarget time

Sequential kills

Target 3

Target 2

Target 1

Range

Retarget time $\propto \dfrac{1}{\text{Slewing rate}}$

θ

Brightness determined by laser power and beam divergence

$B \propto \dfrac{P}{\theta^2}$

- Higher power + narrower beam = longer range, higher kill rate
- Faster retarget time = higher kill rate

dination of the SDIO. Many of the technological breakthroughs of non-SDI projects will offer new promise for SDI.

For any major multifaceted effort such as SDI, some perspective is absolutely essential. This perspective comes in the form of a long-range plan for the project. Although sketchy at this point, there is such a long-range plan for the Strategic Defense Initiative. This plan is really a four phase outline of where the project is headed. Phase one is a research-oriented program and will last through the early 1990s when a decision will be made (by a future president and Congress) either to engage in full-scale deployment or to follow some other option. Clearly, the SDI project is in the midst of phase one. Before a deployment decision can be recommended, the required technology would need to be available to achieve deployment.

In phase two, the systems development phase would be undertaken. The majority of effort in this phase would be engineering rather than experimental (as in phase one). A specific plan, including detailed mission and performance envelopes for each component of the defense, would be completely defined. Further, the most cost effective technical approach would have to be selected and incorporated in the plan.

Phase three would be a phase of transition—a period of incremental, sequential deployment of the defensive systems. The deployment phase would be designed so that each increment would add to the capability of the defense system. More importantly, each increment would be designed to enhance deterrence and as a result, reduce the risk of nuclear war. Theoretically, phase three could be jointly managed by the United States and the Soviet Union. This joint management of deployment would be the result of successful negotiations between the two nations. However, and probably more likely, should the Soviets not choose to cooperate with the US the deployment could proceed with their concurrence.

The fourth and final phase would be one of complete deployment of the defense system. Once completely operational, the system could be fine tuned into a highly effective multilayered defense system. More importantly, the defense system may be used as a negotiating point to first reduce and, hopefully, then eliminate altogether the levels of offensive ballistic missiles of both the United States and the Soviet Union.

The obvious key to the success of phase one is some method to measure progress in the short term—specifically over the next five or six years. To meet the requirements of the early 1990s decision milestone, the short-range program has as its building blocks two basic elements. First is a program to establish the technology base. Over 50 percent of the scientific work for the Strategic Defense Initiative effort will fall into this technology base category. The scientific work is comprised of both basic and applied research involving relatively straightforward extensions of existing technology. The technology base effort is intended to foster the birth of many innovative ideas. Further, the purpose for this base effort is also to provide the framework of knowledge needed to pursue integrated experiments and provide expanded oppor-

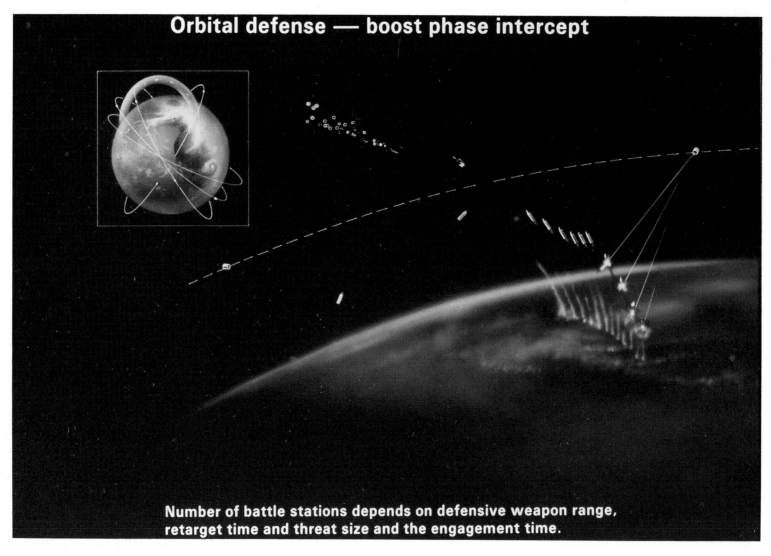

Orbital defense — boost phase intercept

Number of battle stations depends on defensive weapon range, retarget time and threat size and the engagement time.

Boost-phase interceptors require intensive 'look down/shoot down' capability; the illustration *above* demonstrates how such a system may work. The illustration *opposite* states and exemplifies the advantage of boost-phase defense versus mid-course defense.

tunities for faster program growth (particularly in those scientific disciplines which might have far reaching impact).

The second element of the short-range program is one of major experimentation. This includes both experiments for the integration of technology as well as projects to demonstrate capabilities. In order to focus and integrate the information developed out of the technology base, key projects have been chosen which are designed to provide the necessary proof-of-feasibility of the critical elements of a strategic defense system. Proof-of-feasibility experiments tend to be moderately expensive and are driven by time urgency. These experiments are intended to show, early on in the research effort, the feasibility of a key technology with potentially high payoffs. Because these experiments tend to be somewhat expensive, they are often carried out in parallel with other similar projects whenever possible as a way of lowering the risk (cost exposure) of these technically ambitious projects. The emphasis (on which projects to pursue) is on those which offer the possibility of the early resolution of a major issue and which could have a substantial impact on the success of the long-term plan.

Some of the experiments in this category include:
- Development of new infrared sensor materials
- Study of lightweight shielding material to protect both boosters and spacecraft from laser attack
- Research into large structures to be used in space

- Integration of a high power free-electron laser and beam director
- Study of a spacebased neutral particle beam accelerator and sensor package
- A booster-tracking and weapon platform pointing experiment.

Experiments to prove potential system capabilities are the next step beyond showing technological feasibility. These experiments involve technology that has already been demonstrated as feasible and which can be integrated with other system components. Although these experiments tend to be costly, they are valuable in that integration and testing offer ways of avoiding more costly mistakes which could occur due to premature decisions in developing more complex integrated concepts. Premature decisions could (because of mistakes) force the technology base into an excessively lean posture. If this occurs, then the technological risk for the remaining projects may become unacceptably high. In other words, there may be limited flexibility with which to perform alternative tests to assure the success of phase one of the Strategic Defense Initiative project.

Obviously, a project of this size and complexity requires a significant level of funding. Indeed, the research phase of the SDI project was originally set at a cost of about $26 million over a five to seven year period. Major budget reductions imposed by Congress have reduced the planned cost to about $14.5 million for the period 1985 through 1988.

The investment of program funds is a strategy intended to first, protect the technology base; second, increase the emphasis on proof-of-feasibility experiments in order to encourage innovation and push the limit of technology; and third, decrease the number and scope of projects designed solely to demonstrate technical capability. Hopefully, this strategy will give the United States the ability to build a defense system which would work reliably and at a reasonable cost. The diversity of components required will test even the most liberal of thinkers. There will need to be constant attention to priorities and costs. The SDI program can afford neither to pursue 'science for the sake of science' nor to proceed with risky experiments based upon an inadequate technology base.

The key to the success of the investment strategy is the ability to incorporate multiple research paths to satisfy various components required for successful defense system architectures (thus avoiding critical point failures). There is of course the risk of budget reductions. Reductions limit potential alternatives, and should selected options prove unsuccessful, these reductions have the effect of not allowing the SDI to fund 'fall-back' technologies as a way of minimizing financial risk.

This priority-setting has caused the investment strategy to be logically divided into basic elements. These elements are 'hardware' technology programs (such as directed-energy weaponry; kinetic energy weaponry; surveillance, acquisition, tracking and kill assessement; and survivability, lethality, and key technologies). The second element of the investment strategy is the 'software' programs (such as Systems Analysis, Battle Management and Countermeasures). Final-

ly, the remaining elements of investment involve ancillary areas which address threat projections, countermeasures and an activity to stimulate innovaton in science and technology.

The actual Strategic Defense Initiative Organization appropriations and funding requests for the period 1985–1988 were as follows (in $ millions):

Category	1985	1986	1987	1988	4 Year total
Surveillance, acquisition, tracking and kill assessment	$546	$856	$1262	$1558	$4222
Directed-energy weapons	378	844	1615	1582	4419
Kinetic energy weapons	256	596	991	1217	3060
Survivability, lethality and key technologies	108	222	454	524	1308
Systems Analysis and Battle Management	100	227	462	564	1353
Management	9	13	17	18	57
Construction	–	–	10	48	58
TOTAL	$1397	$2758	$4811	$5511	$14,477

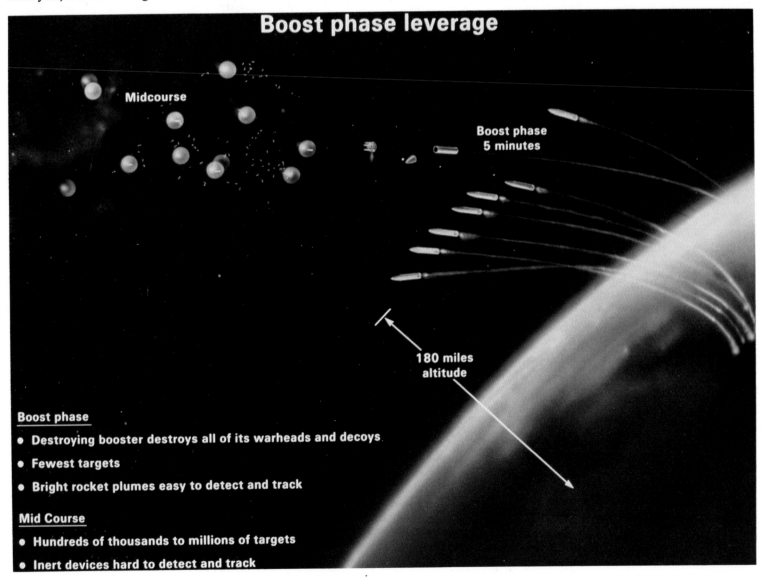

Boost phase leverage

Midcourse

Boost phase
5 minutes

180 miles
altitude

Boost phase
- Destroying booster destroys all of its warheads and decoys.
- Fewest targets
- Bright rocket plumes easy to detect and track

Mid Course
- Hundreds of thousands to millions of targets
- Inert devices hard to detect and track

THE STRATEGIC DEFENSE INITIATIVE ORGANIZATION APPROACH

Since the Strategic Defense Initiative is a fundamental research program, the SDIO should not at this still early date prejudge which defensive concepts are or are not technically feasible. With this in mind, the program managers cannot yet have a fixed SDI system architecture designed. In fact the architecture will most likely evolve as advances are made in the individual research programs.

A system cannot be designed without some basic, common orientation. The members of the Strategic Defense Initiative Organization need to know (at least conceptually) how the architecture will look and how the components will need to interact. Such a conceptual design is necessary simply in order to understand the technical requirements of the system. Further, a conceptual design is useful in defining the systems issues which require resolution either through actual ground testing or simulation.

Because SDI is still in a research phase, program designers are analyzing a number of design options for the system—each involving the basic components of a ballistic missile defense. These defense components are surveillance, weaponry, command control and communications. Although the study process is straightforward, the analysis effort could very well be quite complicated. Each possible system is designed to satisfy a potential threat scenario. Therefore, each system design must include a hypothetical structure as

well as a proposed strategy for operation. Each system design is intended to identify and resolve defense issues.

The systems analysis process begins with a possible defense system design. The various technologies currently under study are then integrated into the proposed design, and we have an alternative which may or may not achieve the mission of the Strategic Defense Initiative (that is, deterring nuclear war through an effective system of defense).

Analysis of the various alternative system designs also requires performance testing. Various tactics on the part of an aggressor as well as a defender must be considered. On the offensive side for instance, the system must be able to withstand suppression attacks. On the defensive side, the system must be configured to optimize the overall performance of the defense.

In conducting these analyses, the SDIO must address three basic defense issues (as defined by Congress in the 1986 Appropriations Bill). First, 'What probable responses can be expected from potential enemies should the Strategic Defense Initiative (SDI) programs be carried out to procurement and deployment, such as what increase may be anticipated in offensive enemy weapons in an enemy's attempt to penetrate the defensive shield by increasing the numbers of quantities of its offensive weapons?' Second, 'What can be expected from potential enemies in the deployment of

weapons not endangered by multilayered ballistic missile defenses, such as cruise missiles and low trajectory submarine-launched missiles?' Finally, Congress wants to know 'the degree of the dependency of success for Strategic Defense Initiative upon a potential enemy's anti-satelite weapons capability.'

The testing effort of pitting system designs against predictions of potential responses by an aggressor is certainly an intimidating and extraordinarily difficult problem. Any deployed defense system would be required to operate against a variety of threat types and force levels. That defense system, however, must be capable of meeting the full spectrum of threats which might emerge over its operating lifetime. Stated differently, not only must the SDIO design be a defensive system, it must also have a comprehensive understanding of real and potential offensive threats available to any aggressor.

The Strategic Defense Initiative Organization has adopted a two part program to satisfy the requirements of Congress. First, the SDI program will include (with the help of the various United States intelligence communities) responsive threat assessments of potential aggressors. This threat assessment includes analysis of offensive ballistic missile attacks as well as suppression attacks on any proposed future defensive system operated by the United States.

Above: This land-launch test of a McDonnell-Douglas Harpoon missile demonstrates that we have progressed far beyond the age of howitzers and '24-pounders.' The Harpoon, one of the latest naval warfare weapons, is normally a 'ship-to-ship' missile.

The second element of the SDI program to respond to the congressional request is the establishment of 'Red Teams.' In order to maintain design objectivity, these Red Teams have been formed to examine and assess independently technical countermeasures to proposed strategic defense systems and technologies. In addition, several Red Teams have been established to develop and evaluate countermeasures to specific system elements and components. The countermeasures developed by the various Red Teams are then presented to Blue Teams which will then consider their impact on the SDI system or the component under consideration. The Blue Teams will propose ways to lessen the effect of the Red Team countermeasures. Ongoing Red Team/Blue Team interactions ensure that countermeasures (both offensive and defensive) are an integral consideration in all stages of the Strategic Defense Initiative research and design process.

The Red Teams' analysis efforts are very useful since they identify credible countermeasures to defensive systems. They are also able to identify countermeasures which are less credible for one reason or another (the reasons can vary from technical to economic to military difficulties). All of these

Red Team ideas are essential to the SDI systems designers. The more credible threats are useful in designing a system which has anticipated the most likely countermeasures (and studying less credible countermeasures is also beneficial). If a countermeasure is not a likely possibility because of technical or economic (or even political) limitations, defense designers need not waste precious time and resources on developing possible responses.

Most importantly, the Red Team/Blue Team concept gives objectivity to the design. By separating the responsibility for conducting defense system design from the countermeasure analysis process, some design independence and integrity is maintained. This division of responsibility ensures that the countermeasure threat analysis is not constrained in any way by the vested interests (conscious or subconscious) of the system designers.

The overall approach of Red Team/Blue Team interaction, combined with up-to-date intelligence analysis, is designed to assist the Strategic Defense Initiative Organization in not only building an effective system design but also in understanding the possible technical responses (countermeasures) to a particular system structure or individual component. This approach will ensure that realistic countermeasures and possible systems threats are continuously applied to the proposed defense system elements, so that any resultant strategic defense could be depended upon to operate successfully in whatever hostile environments an aggressor may wish to create.

A major Red Team/Blue Team effort was conducted during 1984 and 1985, for example. A Red Team was established

Each Minuteman silo room (*left and below*) controls 10 silos, and has backup controls for one other silo room. The 'firing button' actually consists of two widely-separated ignition key switches, a safety precaution which requires two men and two keys to 'fire' the missiles.

to evaluate countermeasures to a proposed High Endoatmospheric Defense System (HEDS). The Red Team effort, in two phases lasting for nearly 10 months (June 1984 through March 1985), concentrated on countermeasures against the defense system.

Beginning in November of 1985 (six months into the effort), a Blue Team was formed to assess the Red Team countermeasures analyses. Finally, an Umpire Team was formed in March of 1985 to review the HEDS Red Team countermeasures and Blue Team countermeasure responses. The Umpire Team was required to develop recommendations about each threat and response. The recommendations were to be of three basic types. First, if credible, include the countermeasures in the HEDS threat assessment. Second, if not realistic, disregard the countermeasure. Finally, if a threat could be further developed, require the Red and Blue Teams to perform additional analyses and sharpen the results.

At the completion of the first phase of the assessment effort, the Umpire Team considered a set of 28 countermeasures identified by the Red Team. The Umpires assessed each of these 28 countermeasures in terms of technical risk, effectiveness and offensive confidence that the countermeasure would work. Based upon this assessment, the Umpires recommended that the Blue Team should develop a response to 15 of these countermeasures.

The Blue Team effort, in addition to responses to countermeasures proposed by the Red Team, included a determination of how well the High Endoatmospheric Defense System needed to perform in order to achieve the defensive goal. Finally, the Blue Team developed specific defense responses to counter the countermeasures developed.

The Strategic Defense Initiative Organization is confident that the Red Team/Blue Team process has resulted in an improved understanding of the possible system countermea-

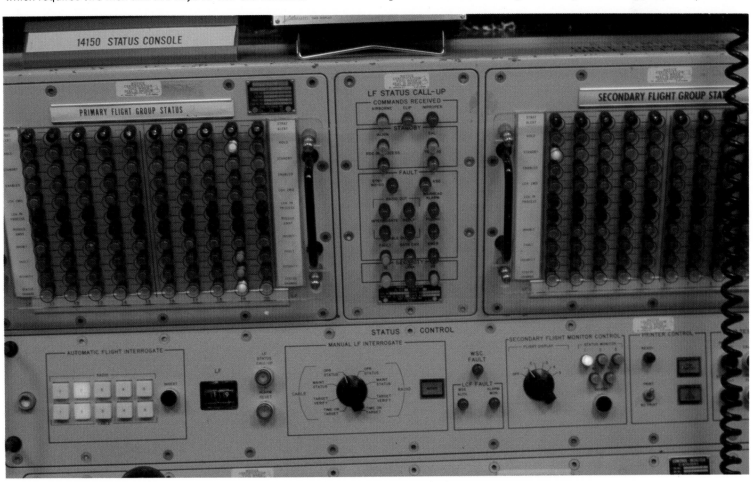

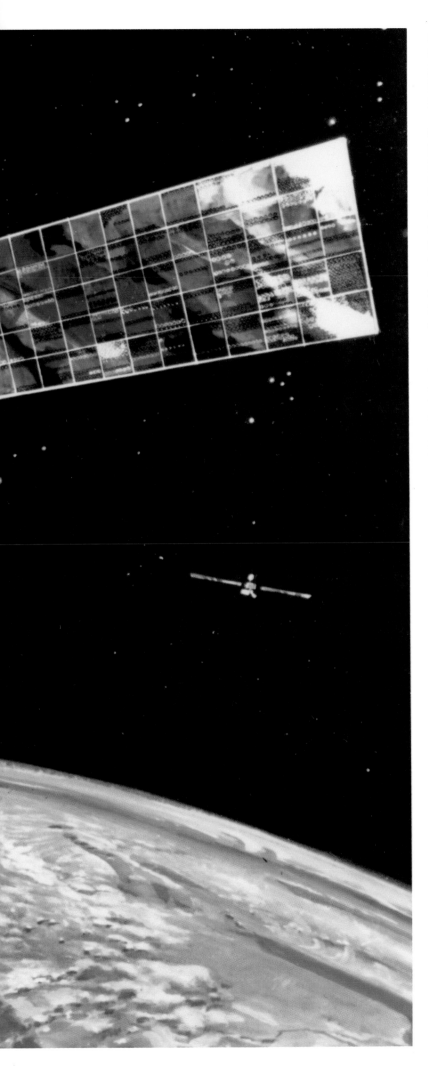

sures available. This process is a systematic, thorough and well-tested method for verifying design concepts. New ideas for countermeasures and countermeasure responses have been identified, evaluated and considered for possible inclusion in the High Endoatmospheric System Design.

The thorough Red Team/Blue Team analysis of the effectiveness of a potential defense architecture (such as the High Endoatmospheric Defense System) leads to a definition of technical requirements of the various subsystems which comprise the overall system. In addition, this analysis identifies key issues (either technical, economic or political) which must be resolved in order to make the defense work. The technology system issues are obviously the easiest to resolve through some combination of ground test, field test and simulation. Clearly, the focus of the SDI is research and design; therefore, the SDIO must satisfy the technical performance requirements established by the various system designers and resolve any key issues which are associated with those designs.

As has been stated, the objective of the Strategic Defense Initiative is the pursuit of several defense system design alternatives and the development of advanced technology concepts which could form the basis for future design alternatives. As a basic research program, SDI is not free to judge which defensive concepts are technically feasible and which are not. As a result, the SDIO cannot simply select a particular design for a defense system. Rather, design alternatives must be established, based upon either existing technology or expected future advancements and then tested against the Red Team/Blue Team efforts.

In order to provide some conceptual understanding of the architectural options which are available, the Strategic Defense Initiative Organization has developed three defense design examples. These sample designs each provide options to engage a ballistic missile during the boost, postboost, midcourse and terminal phase of its trajectory.

The first of these sample defense system architectures is centered around a non-nuclear groundbased and spacebased design. In this example, a series of boost-surveillance satellites would serve as an early warning alert system. This satellite series, in addition to detection of missile launches, would provide an initial assessment of the track of the missiles detected. In addition to the alert system, a second set of satellites would be required for a space surveillance role. This system would provide essential acquisition, tracking and discrimination of potential targets for the defense system. Because this series of satellites is so essential to the success of the entire system, they must be defended, and there must be a sufficient number in orbit to survive a potential defense suppression attack.

With adequate tracking of the offensive threat, spacebased kinetic kill vehicles would engage the targets somewhere along the trajectory. These kill vehicles would be designed to attack all boosters and reentry vehicles and would be dispersed over many different orbiting platforms to counter possible suppression attacks on the defense. These kinetic kill vehicles must be capable of defending themselves—as well as other space assests—from potential spacebased threats.

SDI-oriented concepts include spacebased, boost-phase and mid-course tracking and surveillance sensors such as the artist's concept *at left.* Such sensors would enable detection, tracking and discrimination of all objects in low Earth orbit, including ballistic missile warheads, decoys and debris.

Above: Los Alamos Labs' Radiofrequency Quadrapole (RFQ) rail gun. *At right:* This is a photo of the DOD low frequency laser tracking test conducted on 10 October 1985. Two lasers were used to track a sounding rocket, to determine atmospheric distortion of laser beams.

To counter this defense system an offense may try to attack the defense system directly. This would of course eliminate any possibility of advantage, as the element of surprise would be gone. An aggressor may also attempt to shorten the burn time of its ballistic missile booster, which would in turn depress its trajectory in the hopes of diminishing the effectiveness of the defense. Finally, an offensive threat may be concealed with so-called penetration aids (dummy warheads) in an attempt to simply overwhelm the defense.

Although these offensive countermeasures could conceivably be effectively deflected by a spacebased kinetic kill vehicle, directed-energy weaponry could provide an additional degree of confidence in the defense system. The addition of directed-energy weapons would augment the capabilities of kinetic kill vehicles, particularly in cases where there is reduced engagement time, such as in a low trajectory attack. Directed-energy weaponry might also be used to modify the behavior of incoming targets so that the defense system could classify each as either a threat or a penetration aid. At this point, the neutral particle beam and various types of lasers show real promise in this sort of target discrimination.

Finally, in the case where some threats leak through the various system layers, some sort of terminal defense must be available. Two types of groundbased interceptors show promise for this terminal defense. One operates against threats in the exoatmospheric and high endoatmospheric regions. The other would operate in the mid-to-lower endoatmospheric areas. Both types would require the use of airborne sensor platforms for the most effective defense.

The total number of spacebased elements for this defense system example is likely to be relatively small since directed-energy weapons have very high kill rates. An aggressor could choose to concentrate an attack on the spacebased assets of a defense system. However, the combined effectiveness of directed-energy and kinetic weaponry would provide a strong deterrent against such an attack. To destroy

such a defensive system, an aggressor would be required to pay a high price (sacrifice many weapons in order to overwhelm the defense).

Another defense system architecture example is based around primarily groundbased weaponry. This defense system consists largely of midcourse and terminal kinetic energy weapons with a relatively small number of surveillance satellites. The surveillance satellites would fill the role of missile boost-phase alert and initial tracking assessment. The primary reason for consideration of this exclusively groundbased weapons system is because it relies on active defense elements not deployed in space (thereby lowering system costs), and because it could be very effective in situations where the offense is limited.

The midcourse defense layer of this defense system would require the use of high altitude probes (launched upon notification of boost-phase alert) to initiate exoatmospheric engagements at long range. The terminal tier functions of this defense system would be similar to the previously discussed defense system. However, because there is no boost-phase intercept capability in this particular architecture, the groundbased systems must be deployed in larger numbers to compensate.

This groundbased defense system may be supplemented by directed-energy devices. Recent technological developments show that directed-energy weaponry may provide a performance growth potential by adding a boost- and midcourse-phase intercept capability called 'pop-up DEW.' These directed-energy weapons would be groundbased and

At left: This is a Los Alamos labs conceptualization of a neutral particle beam defense weapon in action against hostile ICBMs. *Below:* This North American Aerospace Defense Command radar station is the heart of a vast early warning radar system.

launched on threat alert. Pop-up DEW could significantly ease the midcourse tracking problem through the effective discrimination of threat targets from penetration aids.

The third example of a defense system is one which addresses the allied defense concept in which the United States and its allies are protected by existing and supplementary new defensive deployments which would provide coverage against shorter-range threats. The unique system architectural requirements for allied defense are determined by three factors: the first consideration is the differing threat characteristics for US allies (the much shorter distances from launch to target require a much quicker response time); second, the diverse variety of targets which requires an assessment of the strategic value of each; and finally, the wide geographic distribution of the potential targets.

The defense system required for the US allies would by necessity, be faster in response. Spacebased early warning and surveillance systems play a key role in the alert stage. Efficient tracking and information support are required for the defense against most shorter range ballistic missiles. Short-range threats with reduced engagement time require additional quick response layers on the part of groundbased defense systems to achieve the desired reduction, if not complete elimination, of offensive missiles. One of these layers would be long-range exoatmospheric and endoatmospheric interceptors. A second layer of defense would be deployed near the forward edge of the territories defended to protect against the shorter-range threat. This area would be protected by an interceptor capable of engaging shorter-range ballistic missiles as well as the threat of atmospheric weaponry such as the cruise missile. Finally, the lowest layer in this defense system would be an airborn fire-control engagement management system which is required to max-

imize the line of sight coverage and monitor engagement performance and kill assessment during a threat.

The actual final design for the Strategic Defense Initiative system architecture will likely involve components from all the aforementioned examples. Whatever the final design in terms of individual components, a system which satisfies the objectives of SDI will need to address the relative strengths and weaknesses of each general type of system. For instance, a defensive system which is designed to operate only in the late midcourse through terminal phases can only accommodate a limited number of defense layers. As a result, the system will not be able to provide the very low leakage required for significant protection of the United States and allied nations from particularly large threats.

Even though it is too early to make a final selection of the overall defense system architecture, the Strategic Defense Initiative Organization does have a current working model. This consists of approximately seven layers of defensive interceptor systems. In concept, each layer would be designed to permit no more than 20 percent of the offensive targets to pass through.

This architecture requires two layers of weapons to attack missiles in their boost phase. One of the layers would consist of directed-energy weapons while the second would be of a kinetic energy nature. The next three layers of weapons would be used to attack threat warheads in the midcourse phase. As with the first two layers, the third and fourth would consist of some assortment of kinetic and directed-energy weapons. The fifth layer would be based on new technology such as groundbased lasers or devices which fire masses of pellets or aerosols. The final two layers of defense would be made up of groundbased rocket interceptors which would contend with any warheads through to the terminal phase.

Below: Nuclear missile-carrying submarines of the US fleet pack quite a punch. Here, a MIRVed Trident missile erupts from the ocean's surface during a Navy test. *At right:* In this artist's conception, chemical laser defense weapons 'kill' hostile ICBMs.

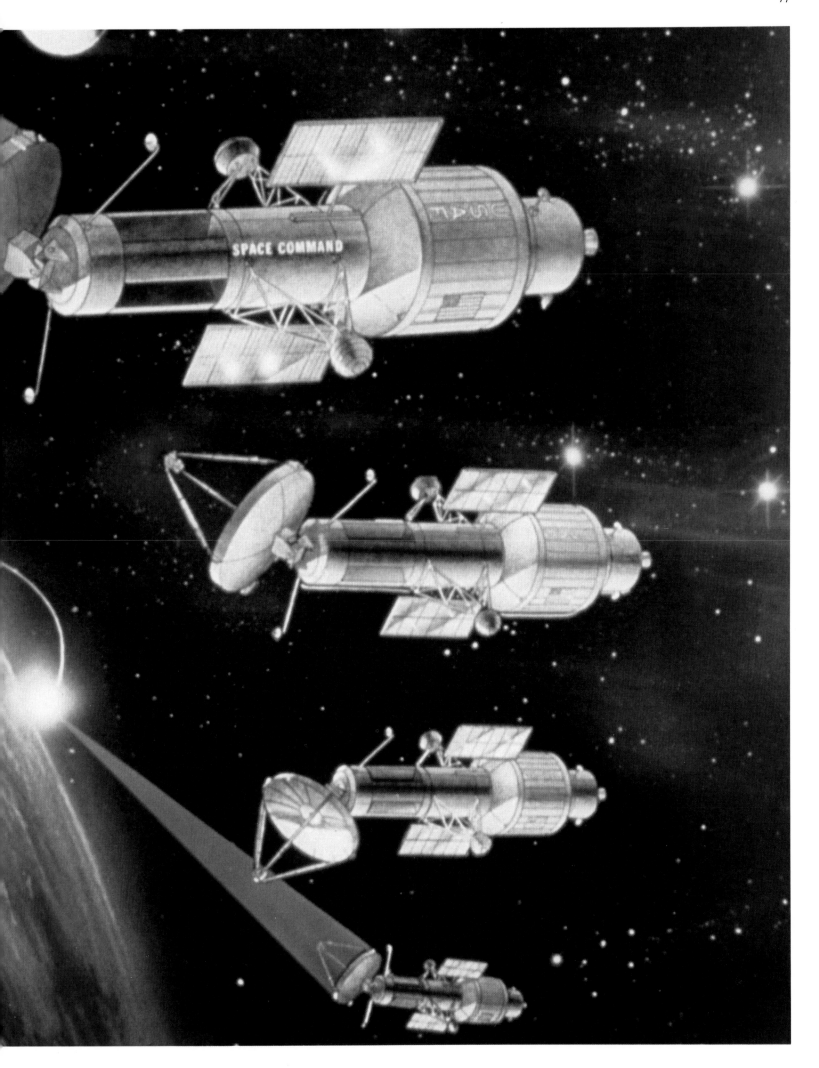

BM/C³ FOR THE STRATEGIC DEFENSE INITIATIVE

No matter what the type of defense system recommended by the Strategic Defense Initiative Organization, and no matter what the mix of groundbased and spacebased hardware, the success of any defense architecture will be based upon its computers, communications and battle management systems. Before reviewing the hardware which is the more newsworthy asset of the SDI, it is appropriate that the behind-the-scenes systems be examined first.

At the rate at which relevant technologies (such as sensors, weapons, communications and computing) are developing, a strategic defense system established in the first decade of the twenty-first century could provide a significantly effective defense. This defense would have the capability to deter an aggressor because there would be no assurance of the success of a potential attack. To be effective, however, such a system would require constant upgrading in order to reflect technological advances and respond to any changes in the threat situation (in other words, to keep the system current). If a decision is made to develop and deploy such a strategic defense system, that system must be capable of continuous evolution in the area of system software.

To understand the complexity of the task at hand, we must review the physical characteristics of the strategic defense problem. The physical dimensions of the battle management problem are threefold. A ballistic missile can be first in-

tercepted during its boost phase. During this phase, which can last for several minutes, a ballistic missile emits enormous amounts of energy with a distinctive spectral signature. During this phase the missile is a relatively large and fragile target which is also easy to detect and locate. At the end of the boost phase, the missile releases what is known as a 'bus' which contains as many as 10 reentry vehicles plus target decoys. During the release, the bus launches the reentry vehicles and decoys, each into a slightly different ballistic trajectory. From a defensive standpoint, the best opportunity to intercept an offensive threat is while the missile is in the boost stage before the bus has released its reentry vehicles and decoys. Not only are the targets large, but considering the number of potential targets contained in a bus, the interception task is much simpler before the bus releases its cargo.

During the midcourse phase, the reentry vehicles and decoys each follow their own unique ballistic trajectory. Depending upon the launch site and target, this midcourse phase can last from 20 to 30 minutes. If a large number of missiles—100 for instance—were launched with each containing as many as 10 reentry vehicles (warheads) and 10 decoys, a defense system would need to track on the order of 2000 targets. Obviously, the ability to distinguish reentry vehicles from targets is a definite requirement for a defensive

system. If the heavy reentry vehicles and light decoys are not correctly distinguished and destroyed during the midcourse phase, they will continue on course and reenter the atmosphere. During this reentry period the decoys will begin to tumble and burn (because they are lighter), leaving only the reentry vehicles to intercept.

The terminal phase of a ballistic missile trajectory—from reentry to target site—may last as little as 40 seconds and leaves little time for an adequate defense. To complicate matters further, a defensive system must expect that submarine-launched ballistic missiles, because of their low trajectories, have no midcourse phase whatsoever. Because of proximity to the target, missiles can proceed from boost to terminal phase quite quickly. In other words the defense must be capable of defending against both the long- and short-range terminal threat.

No matter what mix of weapons and layers of weapons, all the defensive system resources must be tied together with a communications system that will operate under the control of a battle management system. The issues related to battle management, commands control and communication (BM/C³) we will now consider.

Historically, the pattern for the acquisition of weapons systems has been to acquire the weapons first, and later figure out how to devise an effective command, control and communication system. This method, although inefficient, has been reasonably effective for systems of limited scope. But consider the system required for SDI: a global network of sensors which are able to detect offensive threats, communicate an alert, calculate an initial trajectory and track targets. The magnitude of the BM/C³ task seems enormous. Clearly, to meet the SDI objectives, the BM/C³ system must be a prime consideration during the entire research and development period of the project.

According to the Strategic Defense Initiative Organization's Panel on Computing in Support of Battle Management, the most plausible organization for a strategic defense battle management system is what are known as hierarchic. In other words, the communication and information processing structure can be portrayed graphically in a 'tree' diagram. The tree structure of an SDI defense system would have command authorities at the main 'trunk' and 'branches' which lead to weapon and sensor subsystems. A hierarchic system such as this would sense information at the 'leaves' of the tree, analyze it and pass on relevant data toward the trunk. Once command authority has reviewed the information received, commands may be issued and communicated back toward the leaves.

Bringing an example a little closer to reality, we may consider the sensor and weapons parts of a strategic defense system to be much like well-defined subsystems, much like computer peripheral devices. Although these sensors and weapons can be expected to have self-contained computational resources for such tasks as signal processing, aiming, message processing and self maintenance, they would not have any responsibility for coordinating their actions with those of other resources or for allocating resources. For example, a sensor subsystem might have the ability to accept commands to search a given area for a particular signature (such as the emission from a missile during boost phase). The sensor could articulate this command into such suitable action as pointing its sensors, performing the required image-processing operations and reporting the results. The battle management system would then take over and coordinate the rest.

In a system as complex as would be needed to implement an SDI defense, there would be many different types of co-ordination required. Each co-ordination event would have its own purpose, time criticality, and systems benefit. Each type of co-ordination would require more or less involvement of the entire defense system. We can then view the co-ordination events in a sort of importance scale. At the lowest level of importance would be co-ordination efforts such as stereo and other such 'sensor fusion' operational events. This sort of stereo operation would utilize two or more sensors to image a specific objective and obtain more accurate data. At the middle of the co-ordination importance scale would fall such tasks as target discrimination and attack co-ordination. The need for co-ordination here would be to insure as complete a defense coverage as possible as well as to avoid multiple 'shootings' at a specific target.

Intermediate levels on the importance scale would be information of a more global nature. This would include the assignment of priorities on targets in midcourse to insure that areas in the terminal defense would not be overwhelmed. Finally, at the highest levels of the scale would be co-ordination events which would require command and control decisions including putting the system on alert and taking an active defense action (in other words, authorizing weapons to fire at a threat target).

All of these functions are probably easier said than done in a global network of space- and groundbased sensors, weapons platforms and command and control personnel. The defense system will likely always have some sort of change underway (even the orbits of the satellites would likely vary in relation to fixed points on Earth as well as from each other). The battle management system would need to keep track of all the changing patterns. The organization of this effort would likely be in three stages or types of battle groups. The first stage would be an active one; in other words, that particular group of sensors and weapons platforms which are closest to the scene of action. The second stage battle group would be on standby-ready to take over as the orbits of the active group pass away from effective range. Finally, there would be the standdown group which are not involved in any action. Membership in a battle group would

At right: A technician at Norton Air Force Base runs a calibration check on a unit of the Air Force Communications Center radar. *Below:* A USAF Sergeant checks an integrated circuit 'wafer.' The tiniest failure in computer-based weaponry could be trouble.

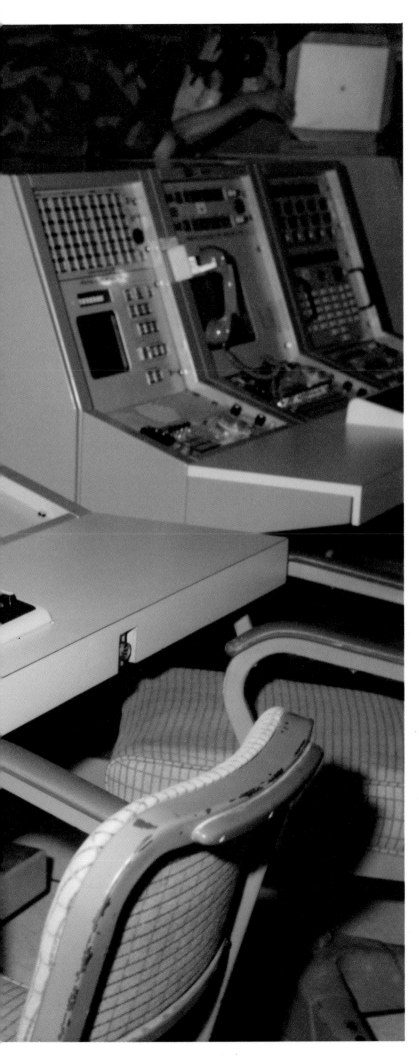

be based on effective proximity to threat targets, so components of the defense system would constantly be coming into and dropping away from the active battle group. To say that any one battle group is dynamic would almost be an understatement. Yet the battle management system would need to have the capability of co-ordinating these defense systems with alacrity.

To do the job, the Battle Management/Command, Control, and Communication system of SDI will require as much—if not more—consideration in planning as do the various weapons and sensor systems. BM/C³ will really be the heart of the entire Strategic Defense Initiative.

The SDI Panel on Computing in Support of Battle Management concluded that the computing resources and battle management software required for a strategic defense system are within the hardware and software technologies which could reasonably be developed within the next few years. However, the panel identified some potential hurdles which must be considered during the research and development phase. These hurdles involved system architecture, software, hardware and communications. We will review each of these potential hurdles before looking at the more well-known elements of the Strategic Defense Initiative (the weaponry and sensors).

The SDIO Panel on Computing studied the issue of BM/C³ architecture carefully and concluded that the battle management system should be an open and distributed system that takes advantage of the special characteristics of the strategic defense system. These special characteristics include such things as operational dynamics, size and the lack of need for global consistency and synchronization.

The Operations Status Display Unit (*at left*) at White Sands missile base is the nerve center of much of the US strategic missile defense system. *Below:* An aerial view of a Safeguard Missile site. The delta array is the missile site radar system.

Global consistency and synchronization are important issues in more conventional distributed systems—such as in banking, for instance. A typical banking system has a global 'state' that reflects every transaction that occurs in a particular period. Each transaction is serialized in order to avoid confusion and to maintain the validity of the global 'state'—a loss of even the smallest transaction could be enough to invalidate the history of the 'state.' The panel determined that a strategic defense system does not have to maintain either global consistency or even a global infinite response state. Given the concept of battle groups, the strategic defense system could distribute its functions while maintaining only central command authority and global situation assessment.

The strategic defense system would require some differing forms of global co-ordination. Three examples of this co-ordination are: first, tight area co-ordination for control of a 'local' battle group. Consider, for example, a small battle group formed by several sensor and weapons platforms which are within a radius of about 150 miles of each other and 100 or so miles above a missile launch area at the beginning of a full-scale attack. The battle management operation of that group would require the exchange of a large volume of information about the location of the missiles as viewed from each sensor. The measurements made by the individual

Above: The US Ballistic Missile Early Warning System at Thule, Greenland. BMEWS systems are very important to both Soviet and US defense.
Right: The Terrier-Malemute sounding rocket which was used in the 10 October 1985 laser atmospheric compensation tests.

sensors could be usefully combined by the group's battle management system in order to provide more accurate tracking of the missiles than could be accomplished by a single sensor.

The second type of control would be that of overall military command control. In other words, a condensed picture of the situations of various battle groups would be necessary for defense assessment. The higher level battle management system would combine threat of assessment information from many local battle groups and various high altitude sensors in order to present a condensed threat assessment to the command authority.

Finally, the third type of control would be loose co-ordination of battle group weapons to individual missiles. The idea would be to optimize, as much as possible, the assignment based on optimal weapons and missile positions. In its strictest sense, this system organization would eliminate the possibility of more than one weapon being fired at the same missile while others are ignored. However, tight co-ordination such as this may not be the best choice. The SDIO has

run simulations which show that a less co-ordinated assignment of weapons would result in only about 20 percent more 'shots' to destroy the same number of targets than would a perfectly co-ordinated system. The SDIO must weigh the benefits of the perfectly co-ordinated system against the cost of much increased software complexity.

In all, the best approach for a defense system architecture would seem to be one of a decentralized nature with varying levels of control and co-ordination. There are many advantages to having an architecture which is decentralized into elements which are capable of independent action. The first advantage is one of simplicity. The less co-ordination of

elements required in the overall system will reduce the complexity of the software. The second advantage is one of evolution. System architectures which are not highly dependent on close co-ordination are more easily changed to incorporate new additions to the defense system or to accommodate new offensive threats. Whatever the ultimate look of the defense system, it will likely scale up from a limited deployment program. A decentralized architecture can scale up with it.

A third advantage is one of diversity. As we will discuss in a following section, the operational software system will probably have some errors built in (they are unavoidable).

Above: These rows of computers are the 'brains' of the North American Air Defense Post, which is inside Cheyenne Mountain in Colorado. Such a precaution as literally using a mountain as a bomb shelter indicates the intensity of today's weaponry.

The key is to force errors in one platform or battle group which would have only a 'local' effect. In other words, if one system part experiences an error, then only that part would be affected. With a highly centralized architecture, the entire system could be affected by one error. This robustness of the system could also be further enhanced by using a variety of vendors and technologies. A decentralized approach would allow the system to be composed of elements that were built and maintained by different vendors. Each vendor would be allowed to employ different hardware and software techniques to develop defense system components. The only requirement would be that all vendors must utilize the same overall system protocols for battle management reporting and control procedures. This diversity in components would make errors more tolerable. Errors or vulnerabilities in one system would not likely be duplicated in others which may be supplied by different vendors.

Finally, a fourth advantage of a decentralized architecture is that of system durability. A loosely co-ordinated system would no doubt be more durable than a centralized system. The magnitude of the defense system and its importance in protecting the peace dictate that the system must work, even in the presence of hardware and software failure. For example, if a system platform loses its data for some reason, we would not want the entire system to go down while that platform is brought back on line. It is much better to keep the system operating while the platform reconstructs its own data from new information.

If a decentralized architecture for the defense system is assumed, we must now face the problem of the enormous amount of computer and communications software which must be written to make the system work. The design of the software for the SDI Battle Management/Command, Control and Communications systems is a mind numbing prospect. Some experts have estimated that the software for this project will require on the order of 10 million lines of computer code! Admittedly, a large number such as this is difficult to comprehend. The lines may be more understandable if we were to equate the lines of code to books. If we assume that each line of code in the defense system software is equivalent to one line on a page in a book, and we further estimate that the average book has 35 lines per page and approximately 500 pages in total, then 10 million lines of code is roughly equal to 571 books—a sizable library!

Once we get past the size of the task, the key software-related question is how to assess the feasibility of the software. Since nothing of this size or complexity has ever been written before, it is likely that several smaller prototype battle management software systems will need to be developed and tested. These different prototypes should probably have different design approaches, so that the project managers may optimize the system performance as much as possible.

Initially, the different prototype projects would work with simulated approximations of the sensor and weapon characteristics. Obviously, each prototype will need to be capable of being expanded into a much larger scale, should more extensive development be warranted. The goal of each prototype battle management system development would be to expand into the development of a deployable system. In effect, these prototype system efforts would be very similar to the hardware (weaponry and systems) research currently underway. This set of projects would equate to a research effort to better determine the most feasible design approach for an effective battle management system. Unlike the weapon and sensor system efforts, there is no real definition of what the battle management system should do. With this in mind, the various prototype efforts will help clarify what is really needed.

This research is an absolute necessity for defense system software. Because of the scope of the task at hand, the effort will require research in a variety of computer software topics. Some of these research topics are worthy of review.

The first area of research is in software testing and maintenance. Because of its inevitably larger size, the battle management task for strategic defense will undoubtedly contain program errors. Given the requirement for a very high level of reliability, how can a system in which errors are first minimized and then tolerated be designed? The first part of the answer lies in the area of system testing. In other words, trying to find ways through simulation to make the system fail. Research in this area will need to produce methods for developing software tests which include a broad range of possible inputs and potential system alternatives (based upon those inputs). Once the system passes development testing and is passed onto a deployment stage (should such a decision be made), ongoing maintenance testing will need to take place. Included in this maintenance effort would be the addition of new components to the system. In short, the maintenance effort would need to be an amalgam of testing and development; almost a never-ending cycle of finding 'holes' in the system and fixing them, while at the same time adding new pieces which must also be tested.

Careful consideration must be given to the problem of how to keep the system error free or at least error tolerant.

Duty at White Sands missile base consists of systems checking (*at left*) and learning codes to convey defense information. A 'Space Operations Center' such as the concept *at below right* would serve both civilian and military ends. *Note* the Shuttle Orbiter.

This consideration must be applied equally to design, deployment, maintenance and evolution testing. The obvious difficulty in the software area is that programmers are limited only by their own ability and the programming language which is used. There is no one right way to accomplish a task and there are varying degrees of success with each software solution. Unlike most of the hardware portions of the Strategic Defense Initiative effort where science dictates the constraints, programming software is an art—a reality or vision interpreted by a programmer. In this environment there will always be a need for system testing and maintenance.

The next major development hurdle for the battle management system is in the area of computing hardware. Unlike the area of software, where advances in reliability are both difficult to believe and foresee, computing hardware holds the promise of continuing rapid progress. Advances in technology are leading to systems which combine increased computing speeds with reductions in size, weight and power requirements. It is more than likely that the strategic defense system, if deployed, will incorporate computers throughout. These computers would be space- and groundbased for actual defense functions including battle management, signal processing and communication functions. There would also be a need for simulation computers for testing. These would be groundbased systems used to simulate the various activities of the battle management system. Because of the

Above: An early conception of the Shuttle Orbiter—which has been considered a distinct advantage in the arena of space defense, as it provides a relatively ready access to orbital regions. *At right:* The flight deck of one of the actual NASA Shuttle Orbiters.

quantity and magnitude of the programming effort at hand, there would need to be computers for software development. Finally, to facilitate computer system design and optimization, there will need to be facilities for hardware development. Experience has shown that the use of computers in the design and validation of custom computer chips has significantly decreased the time required to obtain working chips. The use of computers can be easily expanded to similarly lower defense system concepts.

The United States has a considerable technological edge over the rest of the world in computer hardware technology design and development. In the past we have tended to give up some of that advantage because of delays in applying that hardware in space. However, the Strategic Defense Initiative effort should improve this situation dramatically.

The SDI effort will need to modify somewhat the nature of computer design and development. Defense system computer systems will need to be designed to operate in the hostile environment of outer space for extended periods of time. The problem here is that there are no computer systems of significant power which can operate unattended for several years. As a comparative example, the computers aboard the United States Space Shuttle are designed with a mean time between failures of about 1000 hours (approximately six weeks of nonstop operation). Satellites operating in the strategic defense network will need an operational life of about 10 years (or almost 88,000 hours). Nothing is perfect, however. If hardware faults do occur (for whatever reason), the system will need to degrade 'gracefully' and not collapse, as discussed earlier in the architectural section.

In addition to being designed with long operational lives, these computer assets must also be protected to cope with the potentially damaging attack of an aggressor. For instance, scientists estimate that the high-energy neutron flux resulting from a nuclear explosion would 'erase' (or at least disrupt)

Left: Hughes Aircraft Company's widebody LEASAT military telecommunications satellite was designed to be deployed from the Shuttle Orbiter's large payload bay. *Above:* This is an Orbiter photo of Syncom IV (LEASAT-2), taken after the satellite was deployed from the *Discovery* Orbiter during mission 41-D. *Overleaf:* A NORAD command post.

the information stored in semiconductor memory devices. This high-energy neutron flux could be disruptive from as far away as 600 miles. Therefore, not only must the components be long-lived, they must also be designed with large amounts of nonvolatile data storage systems. Further—if, for whatever reason, the system component does lose its information, it must be able to restart quickly and begin tracking again. With this in mind, certain information which is vital to a restart operation (in addition to restart commands such as time, orbital orientation and function) would have to be designed and stored in a fashion which is immune from just about any kind of upset.

After the problem of architecture, software and hardware have been addressed, we come to the problem of communications. No matter how effective the hardware, or how error-free the software, or how good the architectural design, the success of the information flow rests squarely on communications. The strategic defense system, as envisioned, requires secure, survivable and high-performance communication among all of the defense system assets (both space- and groundbased). The communication capability must be able to cope with any sort of innocent failures, as well as deal with a potentially hostile attack environment (including the phenomena of electromagnetic pulse and neutron flux occurring as a result of a nuclear explosion, jamming attempts and 'spoofing'). Adding to this tall order we must remind ourselves that the defense system assets will constantly be changing position. The relative motion of the individual components (to one another and to the ground) causes the continual rearranging of the various system assets. Since the communication performance requirements are anticipated to be less than a few tens of milliseconds delay among neighboring assets and less than two seconds delay between any remote parties, the communication will likely be centered around high frequencies and limited to line-of-sight connections. With this in mind, the logical configuration of dynamically changing battle groups will cause the line-of-sight communication connectivity to change constantly. The communication system will need to rearrange its messages according to the dynamics of the battle groups. What we have then is a communications network, because direct communications links will not necessarily exist between every pair of system assets which must communicate.

As with most other areas of the Strategic Defense Initiative, much research must be done to achieve the desired communications objective. At this point in time, the existing communication technology probably cannot support the special requirements of the strategic defense system as envisioned. Significant research must be completed in the areas of communication networking, network control, communication protocols and security before a system can be deployed.

In reviewing the requirements, it is possible that the defense system will require a dedicated communications network. On the other hand, communications could well be structured around a dedicated network plus a subnet of other communication satellites. Whatever the choice, there is a need for dense coverage and redundancy, and cost will certainly become a factor.

Once a network scheme is established, it will be necessary to monitor and control (perhaps through simulation) the entire network's behavior including performance, connectivity, activity levels and blockages. It is likely that a communications system simulator will need to be designed and developed in order to validate the selected network design.

Communication protocols are essentially languages which are used to standardize communication information (including message routing, error handling and control). In addition to normal sensor data, the space-borne assets will need protocols to handle immediate—that is, real-time—traffic and priority information. Because there are already some other limited (as compared to SDI) but nevertheless important communications networks already in existence, the defense system communications protocols will need the capability of interfacing with these other networks as well.

Finally, communications security must be carefully considered. Obviously, the security requirements of the strategic defense system are much more severe than those of other systems, simply because of its purpose as well as its unique nature (as envisioned) as an unattended system. At this time existing security systems (in other words—concepts, procedures and devices) are not suitable for the purpose of strategic defense. Again, the need is for research.

No matter what the final make-up of weapons and sensors in the recommended strategic defense system of assets, the real key to making that system work will be the Battle Management/Command, Control and Communications systems (both software and hardware) which will make it work. All of the components will be tied together with a communications system, and all of the components will operate under the control of the battle management system. The considerations in planning which must be made in this area are simply mind-boggling. Objects moving at orbital velocities are traveling sufficiently fast that there must be compensation for speed-of-light delays (when a signal from an orbiting object reaches a sensor which is for example 500 miles away, the object is already almost 100 feet further along the path of its trajectory). Consider further that not only must the battle management system analyze the available information on the object, it must also pass the data along to the other assets of the system and tell those assets where the object is.

There is no doubt that if deployed, the strategic defense system will be a great technical achievement. To make it work, however, the design wizardry and eloquence of the BM/C³ system designers will surely have to verge on genius.

THE DEFENSE CHALLENGE

When President Reagan announced the defense initiative to the world, he was at the same time posing a monumental technical challenge: build a defensive network which would protect us from the threat of a nuclear war. The president's confidence in being able to announce such a program was based on two major assumptions. First, science and technology had reached a point where the challenge was definitely a practical possibility. Second, and perhaps more important, the United States and its allies had the industrial and technological potential to turn the dream of a defense network into a reality.

As discussed earlier, the basic conceptual foundation for the Strategic Defense Initiative came from a Defensive Technologies Study, popularly known as the Fletcher Report. This study laid the groundwork for the research and development effort ahead. Although the report probably did not present any revelations in defense concepts, it did order information in such a way that the possibility of a defense network makes sense.

A ballistic missile defense, if it is to be effective, must be capable of performing six key functions. First, the system must be capable of providing rapid and reliable warnings of an attack at the initiation of that attack. This requires global full-time surveillance of ballistic launch areas. It means that the system must be able not only to detect an attack, but also to determine destination and intensity, and predict likely missile destinations as well as provide information for boost-phase intercept and postboost vehicle tracking.

Second, the defense must be capable of dealing with attacks ranging from a few missiles to a massive, simultaneous launch. The ideal would be to have the ability to attack and destroy missiles in the boost and postboost phases prior to the deployment of reentry vehicles and penetration aids. The ability to respond effectively to an unconstrained threat is strongly dependent upon a viable boost-phase intercept system. For every booster destroyed, the number of objects to be sorted out by the remaining elements of a layered ballistic missile defense system is significantly reduced. Because each booster could be capable of deploying tens of reentry vehicles and hundreds of decoys, the leverage (or the advantage) gained by the defense may be on the order of 100 to one or greater. A boost-phase intercept system is constrained, however, by relatively short engagement times and the potentially large number of targets.

Third, if reentry vehicles and penetration aids are deployed, the defensive system should be able to discriminate and only target the reentry vehicles. This ability to discriminate is intended to make the aggressor pay a high price in mass, volume and investment for credible decoys (the more credible the decoy, the heavier they are; the heavier the

decoys, the fewer actual warheads per missile; and the fewer warheads per missile increases the need for expensive missiles with supporting elements—thereby increasing the cost for the offense). Intercept outside the atmosphere requires the defense to cope with decoys designed to attract interceptors and potentially exhaust the defending force prematurely. The defense does have an advantage of sorts, however. The available engagement time in midcourse is larger than in other phases of a missile trajectory. The midcourse system must provide both early filtering or discriminating of non-threatening objects and the continuing attention to threatening objects in order to minimize the eventual pressure on the terminal system. Interception before midcourse is clearly a more attractive alternative, simply because starting the defense at midcourse accepts the likelihood of a large increase in the number of targets (both multiple independently-targeted reentry vehicles and decoys) deployed.

Fourth, the defense system must be capable of tracking all threatening objects from birth to death (that is, from initial discovery until target destruction). This tracking requirement mandates the unambiguous handover, with few errors, of targets either to designated weapons platforms or to other tracking stations. In short, the system must provide the confidence that all threatening objects are accurately tracked until destroyed.

Kinetic Energy Weapons (KEW) such as the one conceptualized *above* are referred to as 'rocks' due to their use of physical projectiles.

Fifth, the defense system must provide a low cost method for target intercept and destruction during the midcourse phase of its trajectory. The cost to the defense for the interception and destruction of threatening objects must be less than the cost to an aggressor for more warheads.

Finally, the defense system must have the capability to intercept and destroy warheads in the terminal phase of their flight trajectory. This involves the relatively short-range interception of warheads which have made it through various layers of the defense and have begun reentry into the atmosphere. The defended area of a terminal defense interceptor is determined by how fast the interceptor can fly and how easily it can be launched. Terminal defense interceptors fly within the atmosphere and their velocity is limited. Because the terminal defense of a large area requires many interceptor launch sites, this phase of the defense is certainly vulnerable to saturation tactics. It is desirable therefore, to complement the terminal defense with area defenses that can intercept at long ranges. The area of coverage would actually overlap a portion of the midcourse defense.

In each phase of a ballisitic missile flight, a defensive system must perform the fundamental functions of surveillance, acquisition, tracking, intercept and target destruction. Further, it is generally accepted, based on many years of ballistic missile defense studies and associated experiments, that an efficient defense against a threat would be a multitiered defense with each tier requiring all of the capabilities discussed above. Each layer in the defensive system therefore would include some mix of weaponry, sensors and communications capability.

Just as there can be many layers in the ballistic missile defense system, there can also be more than one tier in each of the layers—each layer and tier performing tasks according to its position in the system. Spacebased surveillance, acquisition and tracking components perform different tasks, because the nature of a structured attack changes as the offensive threat objects proceed along their individual trajectories. As each potential reentry vehicle is released from its postboost vehicle (bus), it begins ballistic midcourse flight accompanied by decoys. Each credible object must be accounted for in a birth-to-death track, even if the price of the effort is that many decoys are tracked. Interceptor vehicles of the defense system must also be identified and tracked.

The midcourse sensors have operational requirements which are exactly the same as those in the boost phase. They must be able to discriminate between the threatening reentry vehicles which have survived through the postboost deployment phase, and nonthreat objects such as decoys and space debris from earlier interception and destruction. These midcourse sensors must also provide reentry vehicle position and trajectory information for the eventual firing of defense interceptors as well as target destruction assessement. Reentry vehicles must be recognized, even if there are many false

alarms (such as decoys). The defense system requirements are to track all objects designated as reentry vehicles. Further, the system must also track any other objects which may be confusing to later tiers.

The terminal phase is the final line of defense. In this phase, reentry vehicles have begun to re-enter the atmosphere on their final track toward their individual detonation points. The tasks of surveillance are to acquire and sort all objects that have leaked through the various defensive layers and to identify the remaining reentry vehicles. Whenever possible, target acquisition will be based on information provided by midcourse tracking sensors. In this terminal phase, objects tracked will include reentry vehicles which have been shot at but not destroyed, reentry vehicles never detected and finally, decoys and other objects which were either not destroyed or not discovered. All objects tracked will be handed off to terminal phase interceptors. As can be seen, the terminal defense could be the weakest link in the defensive chain. There are no layers of defense to depend upon—any target which passes through this final layer will result in a nuclear detonation over a predetermined location.

The Fletcher Report was the conceptual beginning for the Strategic Defense Initiative. However, it is now up to the SDIO somehow to fold all the diverse research together into a cohesive program which achieves the objectives of a ballistic missile defense as defined in that report.

Below left: This USAF satellite communications technician is shown operating the AN-TSC-94 satellite communications terminal at Ramstein AFB in West Germany. *Right:* A Titan 3 launch vehicle of the type used to launch such US military reconnaissance satellites as the KH-11, lifts off from Complex 41 at Kennedy Space Center.

6

THE SDI SENSORS

The hardware research and development program was divided into five specific technical programs. These five separate efforts are: SATKA (Surveillance, Acquisition, Tracking and Kill Assessment); DEW (Directed-Energy Weapons); KEW (Kinetic Energy Weapons); SLKT (Survivability, Lethality and Key Technologies); and IST (Innovative Science and Technology). We shall survey each of these important research areas.

The purpose for SATKA research is to investigate sensing technologies that can provide the type and quality of information required to activate the defensive system, manage the battle and assess the status of the system of assets before during and after an engagement. Space, air and ground technologies are being explored to support the SATKA requirement. Although we think in terms of SDI research, the various sensor techniques are probably the most mature technology we have available, as we have had spacebased sensors for more than two decades. Although many of these satellite sensors were for purely scientific purposes, there can be no doubt that the majority of spaceborne sensors were primarily for military applications. Three broad classes of military sensors can be identified. The first are for Electronic Intelligence (ELINT) applications. ELINT involves the study of radar and other non-communication signals. This particular kind of satellite system, also known as a 'ferret,'

The Satellite Control Facility of the Sunnyvale Air Force Station (*far left*) is centered on a building known as the 'Big Blue Cube' (seen *at center* of photo), which is the actual satellite control center for the complex. *Above:* This is an artist's conception of the Astro-DSCS III (Defense Satellite Communications System, Phase III).

has many applications including locating radio transmissions, eavesdropping on communications and monitoring telemetry data from missile tests. The purpose of a particular radar device, for instance, can be determined through the examination of such things as pulse width, the repetition of the pulses and their frequency.

The second form of military sensors in space may be considered Communications Intelligence (COMINT). This particular variety of intelligence includes the interception and analysis of radio communications. The purpose of this form of intelligence is simply to try to determine an adversary's intentions through what is said on the radio. The task is not directed toward picking up individual conversations, but more to look for changes in the pattern of the traffic. For instance, the change in intensity or level of communications chatter between one military command to another could betray an adversary's intention and give our military cause to go on alert status.

A subset of COMINT is what can be called a Signal Intelligence (SIGINT) which really connotes the passive activity of listening and trying to identify the military units and weapons systems of a potential enemy. This sort of study of an opponent's status of forces and equipment could well provide information on the development of new equipment, technologies and tactics.

The third general category of satellites is designed specifically for optical surveillance missions. These sensor packages may include infrared, radar and optical technologies and they are designed to provide military analysts with a picture of some particular Earthbased object or event. For instance, the United States depends on this sort of satellite to detect nuclear explosions anywhere in the world. This sort of mission is aimed at verifying compliance with treaties—the nuclear test ban, for instance.

Missile launches may be detected by this sort of early warning satellite. For example, missiles launched from China and Russia can be monitored by the United States via a satellite over the Indian Ocean. A typical early warning satellite would have a telescope with an array of infrared detectors, each detector scanning an area about four miles across. The science of launch detection may be considered (for SDI purposes at least) a mature technology. The demands of boost-phase detection can undoubtedly be met simply by making steady improvements in the existing technology.

An interesting surveillance method is through satellite photo reconnaissance. These devices utilize a combination of technologies to obtain highly detailed pictures of Earthbased objects. The resolution of pictures taken from satellites is so precise that analysts can measure the size of, and even predict the performance of, an aircraft sitting on the ground.

The United States also operates a variety of photo surveillance satellites. The 'Keyhole' (KH) series of satellites is just one of which many have heard. A currently known version of this series is the KH-11 model which uses digital imaging devices to look down on Earth. This particular satellite has a visual life expectancy of about two years and, because of its multispectral infrared sensors, can 'see' through cloud cover.

Probably the best known United States spy satellite is the model called 'Big Bird.' This series of equipment includes high resolution cameras to 'see the world.' From its location in outer space, this satellite's cameras can identify objects which are as small as 12 inches (the size of a small watermelon). The onboard cameras are used to expose film which can be jettisoned by the satellite. A specially outfitted C-130 Hercules aircraft is then used to catch the film as it falls toward Earth.

Clearly, the SATKA requirements for appropriate sensor operations will be enormously complicated. In some esti-

Each Defense Meteorological Satellite Program (DMSP) satellite (*left*) is a spaceborne sensing technology testbed and global weather station for the US military. *Below:* Technicians track and catalog orbital objects from the Cheyenne Mountain Space Surveillance Center.

mates the number of rapidly moving targets to be identified and tracked could well exceed 100,000. This is further complicated by the fact that the data about each target's probable function must be passed around to various elements in the defensive network rapidly and accurately. If this were not enough, there can be no doubt that an aggressor will work very diligently at fooling or even destroying the defensive systems. Before we look further at the phases of the SATKA requirements, it is necessary that we examine the ways that sensors may be nullified.

Without even considering the number of satellites necessary for the SDI system, it is fair to say that the United States is heavily dependent on satellites. Indeed, it has been estimated that over 70 percent of all American overseas military communications links are relayed through satellites. As our reliance on satellites has increased, so too has our awareness that the loss of satellite equipment due to foreign aggression could be a crippling blow to military readiness.

There are really only two ways to completely destroy a satellite. The first method is definitely straightforward—shoot it down. The vehicle for this particular tactic may be gun, rocket, energy or some other mechanical means. The results are always the same—the satellite is destroyed. A second method of destruction requires brute force, but can also be a bit more subtle. This method relies on what is known as an Electric Magnetic Pulse (EMP).

When a nuclear device is detonated, the blast includes a wave—or pulse—of full-spectrum electromagnetic energy. The almost instantaneous pulse of power could be equal to as

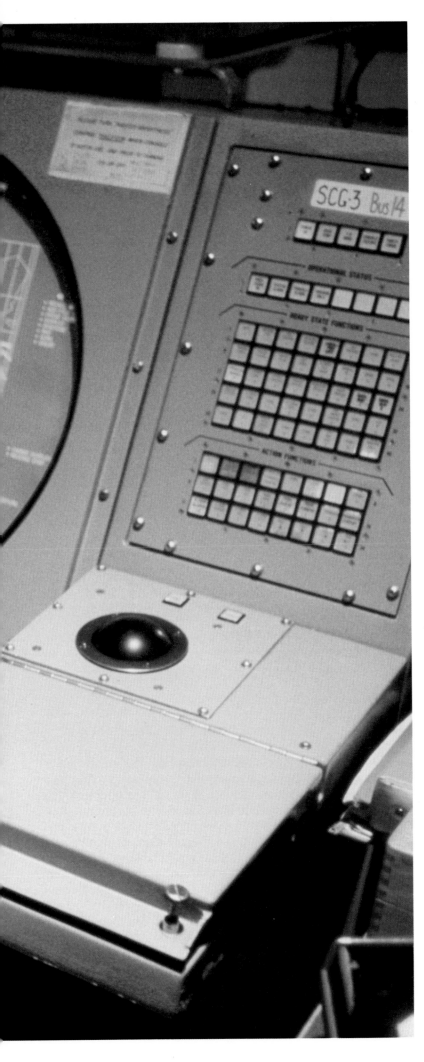

much as five-hundred billion megawatts. This pulse would certainly be sufficient to permanently damage the solid state electronics of a satellite system. The pulse can cause electrical fields which, when introduced into conventional metal oxide semiconductors, alter the characteristics of the device and force a malfunction. These circuits, if they did not fail completely, would certainly behave erratically. Interestingly, as our systems become more sophisticated and faster, the likelihood increases that the EMP will damage the system. Conversely, older and (by definition) simpler equipment based on the outdated tube technology is the least vulnerable to EMP. Depending upon the type of nuclear device, the EMP could travel many miles indiscriminately destroying (or at least disrupting) any electronic systems in its path.

Systems can be hardened against electromagnetic pulse damage. However, this requires the additional expense of encasing the systems in sealed metal boxes which will either absorb or deflect the pulse. In addition to cost, the hardening methods discovered thus far extract the further penalty of weight.

For SDI purposes the various satellite types briefly discussed above will certainly provide the basis for SATKA. Spacebased rocket launch detection sensors will detect the initiation of an attack and provide the initial tracking data to assess the attack, bring boost-phase interceptors to bear and provide data to factor in kill assessment. These sensors must provide rapid and reliable warning of attack as soon after launch as possible. One boost-phase surveillance system which holds promise is the Boost Surveillance and Tracking System (BSTS). Satellites in this system would be set in an orbit which allows fulltime coverage of ballistic missile launch sites. Launch detection will likely utilize infrared functions to detect the heat from the missiles as they are launched. In some repects, this is a relatively simple task. Large rockets have a tremendous fuel flow. The Saturn series of the US missile fleet, for instance, burns about 10 tons of fuel per second. Obviously, ICBMs are smaller but the point is clear—the fuel burned creates a large, easy to spot heat signature which can be readily tracked.

The difference between the expected BSTS and current infared surveillance satellites is centered around tracking ability. The current versions follow the infrared signature of a rocket plume. For targeting purposes, the future satellite systems must be capable of locating and tracking the missile in front of the very hot plume. In the long view, infrared sensors will most likely be used for the initial detection of a launch. Precise tracking of targets and weapon-pointing functions will probably require some form of laser radar.

Before long, the SDIO expects to conduct spacebased BSTS experiments to demonstrate technology capable of upgrading the existing early warning system. These experiments will determine if sufficiently sensitive tracking and signature data can be collected from orbit 'looking' down against the background of Earth. As it could be considered an upgrade of our present early warning system, the experimental device will be limited in capability so that it cannot substitute for an ABM component (which would be a violation of the ABM Treaty), but it is expected to be capable of performing early warning functions (which are permitted by the treaty).

Above left: A USAF technician confirms a sighting he has seen on his tracking screen. The oscillating, parallel lines that we see on the screen are the 'ground traces'—or continuous orbital path, as measured against Earth's surface—of a non-geosynchronous satellite.

The boost phase is a critical time for the defense system. This phase of a ballistic missile track, up until the deployment of decoys and reentry vehicles, lasts a relatively short time, usually no more than a few minutes. During this boost phase, the offensive threat will rise to an altitude of about 300 miles. The first line of defense, the early warning elements of the system, must be tough as well as sensitive. They must have the capability to endure after the boost-phase portion of a battle is completed. Further, the BSTS is essential for launch strength assessment and handover to other defensive elements.

Once ballistic missiles have passed into the postboost and midcourse phases, sensors must provide accurate and efficient tracking and discrimination data about reentry vehicles, light-weight penetration aids, and other debris. This phase of a ballistic missile trajectory is both less time-critical and more complex than the boost phase. The postboost and midcourse phase last much longer than in the boost portion of flight. For intercontinental ballistic missiles, this phase can last up to 30 minutes. However, after the boost phase is completed, the missile releases a bus containing on the order of 10 reentry vehicles and decoys. At a predetermined altitude and velocity, the bus then launches each of these potential targets into a unique ballistic trajectory. During this phase, the reentry vehicles and decoys will reach maximum velocity and an altitude of about 900 miles above the Earth. Obviously, no aggressor would simply permit its

The USAF/Woolridge Defense Support Program Satellite *(above)* was deployed by Shuttle Orbiter Discovery 51-C on 24 January 1985. *Left:* An Atlas 'boosts' a satellite in 1978. *Right:* Beale AFB's PAVE PAW Space Command Center for detecting Submarine Launched Ballistic Missiles.

missiles and satellites to be eliminated by a defender. Without doubt, an aggressor will be prepared to protect its equipment through the use of one or more countermeasure techniques.

Although countermeasures are out of our scope, it is appropriate that we review a few of the techinques which would undoubtedly come into play. The first such technique is communication jamming. Radio links are a prime target for countermeasures, as an opponent can easily block the communication traffic on a given set of frequencies. If effective against a defense system such as SDI, such jamming could quickly bring the network to a standstill. With this in mind, defense system planners will be required to stick to line-of-sight communications and may even consider frequency hopping as an alternative. Jamming of frequency hopping communications links is nearly impossible today. A hostile opponent may be able to detect a short burst of a communication signal on a given frequency. However, the opponent has no way of identifying what the next frequencies in the hopping pattern will be. The only systems which can know what are the next frequencies are those of the defense. No doubt, this sort of frequency-hopping plan will increase the complexity of the defense. However, if the defense is to work properly, it must have secure communication links.

Radar can also be easily jammed by an aggressor. A radar unit sends energy in the form of a signal, toward a target.

This energy bounces off a target and is reflected back toward the radar unit. The problem with radar is that the return signal is significantly weaker than the original pulse of energy. Not only has the signal's journey out to the target and back imposed an attenuation penalty, but a large amount of energy has been lost in the reflection process due to absorption of the signal by the target. Considering the inherent weakness of radar, it is a relatively easy task for an aggressor to 'jam' a radar unit by swamping the genuine echoes with electronic noise. Such jamming can simply overwhelm a radar unit by causing its screen to illuminate to full brightness. At some point, as the target moves closer to the radar unit, the radar signal can 'burn through' the surrounding noise and locate a target. In a battle situation, however, the time it takes for this burn-through could mean the difference between an effective defense and a successful attack.

A more subtle method of jamming is deception—in other words, feeding a radar unit with false data. One very effective and inexpensive deception technique is the use of what is known as chaff. Chaff is made up of small strips of conducting material, cut in various lengths to enhance its reflection of radar energy. Each chaff strand acts as an efficient receiver and retransmitter of the radar wave length to which its physical length is matched. In effect, chaff can trick the radar unit into 'seeing' a target which is much larger than the actual size of a chaff strand. As an example, a small chaff package about the size of a hamburger bun could fool a defending radar into 'seeing' a target the size of a jet fighter or a reentry vehicle. Effectively dispersed, chaff can be used to build up radar-proof corridors through which reentry vehicles may fly almost without fear of detection.

Much of the SDI sensor research is focused on infrared technology in order to avoid the jamming and fooling which would take place with radarbased systems. Modern infrared sensors are passive devices which rely on spotting the heat emitted by objects within a particular field of view. As we have noted earlier, all objects radiate infrared energy. The hotter the object, the greater the energy emitted. Infrared sensor technology can be envisioned as simple television cameras which build up a heat image of a target as compared to a cooler background. The sensors then must rely on sophisticated computer processing to 'lock' onto a designated portion of the heat image.

As simple as an infrared sensor may seem, it too can be jammed or fooled. The first method of jamming is very straightforward: blind the sensor through the use of a burst of laser energy. The heat generated in the sensor would either permanently or temporarily blind the sensor much the way a flash of strong light (strobe, flash bulb, etc) will cause the human eye to see 'spots.' Fears about the possibility of 'blinding' has resulted in the High Altitude, Low Observable (HALO) research program. This effort is designed to produce laser resistant, high resolution sensors which can stare constantly at a target without fear of blinding. Another method for fooling infrared devices is through the use of inexpensive flares to generate bright heat sources.

All things considered, electronic countermeasures can be inexpensive and quite effective. Compared with active jamming techniques, expendables such as chaff and flares could be used in concert to partially disable a defensive sensor

The phased-array antennae of the Sparrevohn Air Force Station (*above right*) in Alaska are important for their communications role, and officially serve as an Air Force Communications Service documentation facility—keeping our 'wires' straight, not crossed.

R2P2 Simulator System Components

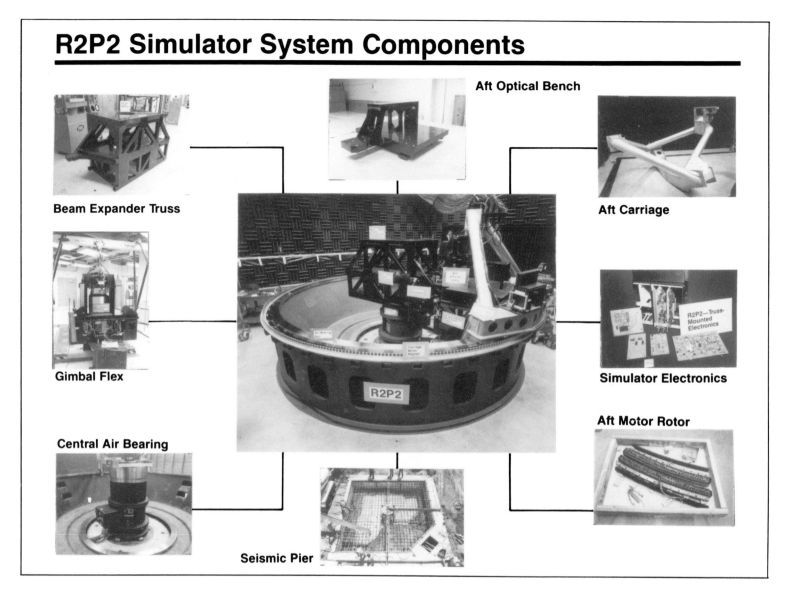

Beam Expander Truss

Aft Optical Bench

Aft Carriage

Gimbal Flex

Simulator Electronics

Central Air Bearing

Aft Motor Rotor

Seismic Pier

system. Certainly, the use of such seemingly crude counter-measures can sufficiently confuse a defensive system long enough to allow a ballistic missile attack to slip through a defense. The midcourse surveillance and discrimination sensors must also track reentry vehicles, decoys, chaff and other debris that constitute the 'threat cloud' released at the end of the boost phase. Sensors are intended to provide data that can help discriminate decoys, chaff and debris from the reentry vehicles carrying the warheads. Further, these sensors will provide the predicted positions of targets to bring the midcourse intercept weapons to bear, as well as assist in kill assessment.

The middle layer of sensors must be capable of accepting track data from boost-phase sensors as well as perform similar acquisition, tracking and processing functions. One concept for this midphase sensor is the Space Surveillance and Tracking System (SSTS). The sensors in this system will also likely be based on infrared tracking technologies. In the near vacuum of space, objects cool rapidly and since decoys have no internal electronics, they will likely cool much more quickly than the actual reentry vehicles. The sensors will simply measure the difference in heat between various potential threat objects and will consider the warmer targets as the likely reentry vehicles. (There are two other ways of discerning decoys from real siarheads through the use of lasers. The first method involves 'tapping' all of the observable projectiles with a burst of laser energy and then measuring how they recoil. The decoys, which are lighter in weight, will be pushed

further by the 'tap' than will the heavier warheads. The second method is more direct. A laser beam of moderate intensity could be directed at all potential targets. The heat from the laser will burn through the thin-walled, relatively fragile decoys and destroy them. This would leave only warheads for the defense to track and kill.)

The SDI research program will experiment on the SSTS concept. The objectives of the experiment are twofold: first, to demonstrate a technology capable of upgrading the current United States Space Detection and Tracking System (SPADATS); second, to permit a decision to be made on the applicability of more advanced ABM technologies. The experiment will demonstrate the capability of the collection of tracking and signature data on a number of space objects against the background of both the earth's upper atmosphere and space. At this time, the SDIO plans to launch a data-gathering satellite for this experiment sometime in the early 1990s. In accordance with the ABM Treaty, the performance capability of this satellite will be significantly less than that necessary for full ABM performance levels, and the system could not be substituted for some future ABM component.

The key element in the ability of the sensors to detect heat is that each sensor must maintain a constant, very cold temperature. Therefore, these heat-detecting infrared sensors must be cooled (even in space) in order to function properly. Special refrigerators called cryocoolers are needed to produce the constant low temperatures for these sensors. The

In concept a modified Boeing 767, the US Army's Airborne Optical Adjunct (*above*) will aid groundbased radar in determining real, from decoy, ICBMs. *Opposite:* Martin Marietta's R2P2 Simulator System is more sinister than George Lucas's R2D2, with which it is not to be confused.

technical challenge in this area is cryocooler life, reliability and performance—and research has been promising. Experiments designed to demonstrate the capability to cool these detecting devices have resulted in almost one year of successful operation at speeds designed to accelerate life testing. For instance, one of the programs absorbed by the SDIO in the development of the Boost Surveillance and Tracking System effort is the High Altitude, Low Observable project which has already produced new infrared sensors. These new sensor devices are sensitive to longer wavelengths because of the new cryogenic cooling techniques and more sophisticated lightweight optics.

The SSTS envisioned for SDI would provide a realtime, spacebased system for midcourse ballistic missile surveillance and tracking. In addition, the Space Surveillance and Tracking System would provide timely satellite attack warning and verification. Depending on what deployment decisions are made for SDI, SSTS also could be the initial front line early warning components of the defense system. As with Boost Surveillance and Tracking System, SSTS must also provide track and target data to postboost and midcourse interceptors. Finally, these sensor systems must be capable of handing offtrack and target data to terminal phase tracking systems.

In the terminal phase, sensors must provide efficient tracking and discrimination of reentry vehicles from penetration aids and other debris. These sensors will be capable of receiving tracking data from the midcourse sensors and, like the sensors in the previous defense layers, this phase will track targets, analyze data and pass commands to a variety of intercept vehicles.

Since this is the final phase of defense, the terminal sensors will need to measure precisely the position and projected track of each threatening object just before committing in-

terceptor resources. The actions of the defense are critical as this terminal phase will cover an area from ground level to about 150 miles in altitude. The velocity of the vehicles at reentry will be such that this phase may last for as little as 40 seconds. The goal for this surveillance phase is, in the few tens of seconds it takes for attacking warheads to enter the atmosphere and deteriorate, to acquire, track and collect data on the behavior of re-entering objects in the atmosphere and to support discrimination, predict intercept points, provide intercept communications and assess kills.

Two interesting concepts, both of which may play a role in the fully developed defense system, are currently being explored by the SDIO. The first of these is the Airborne Optical Adjunct (AOA). This concept is based on a long-endurance aircraft filled with sensor devices. Its systems would be capable of detecting arriving reentry vehicles which leak through the preceding layers of the defensive network. Flying at altitudes of up to 65,000 feet, the AOA sensors mounted on top of the aircraft would be able to peer into space from a vantage point well above the majority of atmospheric disturbances. The AOA would be capable of accepting target 'handoffs' from the SSTS as well as new target detection. AOA sensors would provide all the data necessary to acquire, track and discriminate reentry vehicles. Finally, AOA will provide information to groundbased surveillance systems for the terminal intercept.

A planned SDIO Airborne Optical Adjunct experiment will demonstrate the technical feasibility of long wavelength infrared (LWIR) acquisition, tracking and discrimination of strategic ballistic missiles from an airborne platform in sup-

port of groundbased radar. The plan calls for the initial airborne platform to be a Boeing 767, but the ultimate platform is yet to be determined. As with other experiments, the AOA experimental device will not be capable of substituting for an ABM component due to its planned sensor and platform limitations. Nevertheless, these experiments will validate the technology required to acquire targets optically at long ranges, track, discriminate and hand over to groundbased radar. It will also provide a data base that would support future evolutionary development of airborne optical systems for use in a defense system. As part of the AOA technology verification efforts, wind tunnel tests have been conducted to evaluate the effect of sensor configuration on aircraft performance and to measure the associated wind effects on sensor performance. Initial sensors have been fabricated and are currently being tested.

The final sensor in the defense system could well be the Terminal Imaging Radar (TIR). As we noted earlier, radar detects targets by illuminating them with powerful energy waves and then receiving the reflected energy. There are two basic types of radar—pulse and continuous wave. The more traditional method is pulse, which relies on the echo principle. In other words the radar transmits a brief pulse of energy, shuts down the transmitter and listens for an 'echo.' The speed of the energy is constant (much like light), so by noting the time between sending the pulse and receiving the echo, a target range can be calculated. Continuous wave radar operates over a band of frequencies. Signal frequency is varied with respect to time. The receiver in the radar unit must measure the frequency of the reflected signal, then calculate the time interval which has elapsed since a signal of that particular frequency was transmitted. Once the time interval is known, it is a simple procedure to calculate the range of a target.

In conventional radar units the antenna must be pointed in the direction of the target. The newer systems do not rely on such antenna systems. Instead of using such reflectors, defense radar units will utilize flat plate antennas consisting of arrays of elements called phase shifters. Each phase shifter will transmit a tiny portion of a radar signal, and each fraction of the signal will be delayed by a programmed interval so that an extremely focused beam can be created. Because the degree of phase shift generated by each element in the array can be altered slightly, radar designers can actually 'steer' the beam in a specific direction. This electronic steering essentially eliminates the traditional rotating dish antenna. The new design of flat plate-array radar units has a fixed structure with a beam which is moved electrically to align it with a target.

Cobra Dane is such a phased array device. Located on a small island at the western edge of the Aleutian chain, Cobra Dane is less than 500 miles from the Soviet Union. Cobra Dane has a radar face which is about 100 feet in diameter and can scan an area 120 degrees horizontally and 80 degrees vertically. Cobra Dane is oriented in such a way that it can monitor Soviet missile test ranges. It has been reported that the Cobra Dane radar is so sensitive that it can detect a metal object as small as a grapefruit at a distance of more than 2200 miles. For reference, 2200 miles is approximately the distance between Los Angeles, California and Honolulu, Hawaii. Phase array radars can rapidly switch from one target to another. The time lapse in switching from target to target can be measured in microseconds. Therefore, multiple targets can be tracked almost simultaneously. When in tracking mode, Cobra Dane can simultaneously follow as many as 200 objects at ranges up to 1300 miles.

Terminal Imaging Radars would receive data from the Airborne Optical Adjunct and then provide precision track information for high endoatmospheric terminal phase engagements of the most threatening objects. TIR will be an X-band ABM radar which may be tested in an ABM mode in full compliance with the terms of the ABM Treaty. This fixed, landbased radar will be tested by SDIO at a designated ABM test range. The primary objective of the tests is to demonstrate the performance and effectiveness of an X-band ABM radar. TIR will be permanently installed in an existing radar building and will require this building for its structural support. The radar device, called Cobra Judy, has been installed on the research ship USS Observation Island for further testing and development. The Cobra Judy radar will improve the United States' capability for making measurement on reentry vehicles. Following a short test period, USS *Observation Island* will maneuver Cobra Judy close to the Soviet Union in order to build as complete a data base as possible on the unique characteristics of Russian reentry vehicles. This data collection effort is intended to lead to interpretative data on Soviet ballistic missile elements. The real advantage of such a shipbased radar is that it can legally get close enough to collect data during reentry phases of missile flight. The ultimate use of the data base will be the design and operation of both midcourse and terminal phase radar tracking devices.

In order to accomplish the technical objectives of SDI and to provide the confidence necessary for an early 1990s deployment decision, the SDI Satellite, Acquisition, Tracking and Kill Assessment program operates in three basic ways: technology development—designing the technology to support the defense system concept; experimentation—proving that the technology meets the desired objectives; and collection—building a data base for the interpretation of data on ballistic missile elements. Clearly, SATKA will be enormously complicated. Not only must planners construct an effective network of sensors and battle management techniques, but they must also be prepared to repulse attacks against the system and use whatever countermeasures which may be deployed to fool or jam the system. At this time SATKA research efforts are expanding the technology base in areas such as long wavelength infrared and low light devices, phased array microwaves and ultraviolet radars, optical telescopes and various other detection devices. No matter what the decisions on SDI, the research provides a rich base for new technologies based in space, in the air or on the ground.

Every benefit has its associated problem, however. As we learn more about sensor and communication technology, we will begin to rely more and more on these new devices and techniques. As our reliance on these increase, so might we be crippled if we lose the new capability. For every measure, there is a countermeasure and for every countermeasure, there is a counter-countermeasure. As we evaluate SDI we must constantly remind ourselves that there is no final advantage, there are only interim gains.

The sensors in the various layers and tiers of the defense will be linked by the battle management system to the various weapons of the defense network. These weapons systems, because they seem to be more in the realm of science fiction, have received more publicity than any other part of SDI.

The Directed-Energy Weapons (DEW) technology program of SDI has an objective of identifying and validating the technology for directed-energy systems that can destroy large numbers of threatening boosters and postboost vehicles in the tens to a few hundreds of seconds that the missiles are in their boost phase. This program has the further objective of discriminating midcourse decoys from warheads by probing them with a directed-energy beam that either interacts with the target, scatters radiation from the nuclear warhead or creates other identifying signatures.

These two missions, boost-phase intercept and midcourse discrimination, are the keys for SDI to achieve high levels of ballistic missile defense effectiveness against even the most difficult threats. To achieve its objective, this SDI program must achieve advances in directed-energy science.

Cobra Dane (*above opposite and overleaf*) is composed of 'phased' steerable beam radar antennae. Cobra Dane monitors Soviet missile test ranges from its base in the western Aleutian islands. The research ship USS *Observation Island* (*below*) is the test platform for the Cobra Judy radar system, which will study Soviet ICBM flight characteristics.

BEAM WEAPONS

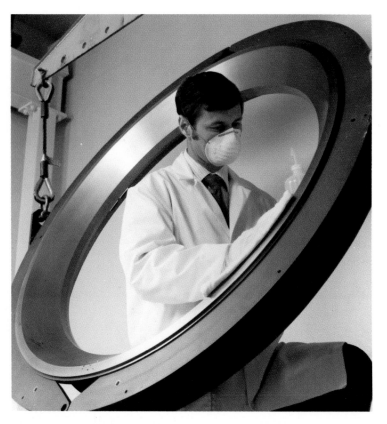

Directed-energy weapons can deliver destructive energy to targets at or near the speed of light. The quick travel to target makes them especially attractive candidates for use against missiles as they rise through the atmosphere. Successful engagement of missiles in these initial phases could allow the defense to destroy missiles before they release multiple warheads on their own independent trajectories. The capability for achieving such a defensive advantage is the key to the SDI concept. Over the long term, directed-energy weapons could hold the key to defeating some of the more stressing threats that might be deployed in response to possible defensive deployments by the United States. These threats include such things as fast-burn boosters which could significantly shorten the exposure time of offensive missiles in their most vulnerable boost phase.

Beam weapons concepts now being studied include spacebased lasers, groundbased lasers using orbiting relay mirrors, spacebased neutral particle beams and endoatmospheric charged-particle beams guided by low power lasers. In addition to research on beam generation technologies, advancements are also sought in beam control; optics; fire con-

At left: A USAF technician polishes a high energy laser's rear cone mirror. The Sperry Corporation submits this conception (*above*) of a directed-energy weapon hovering in space, waiting to mirror the sun, which is here just clearing the Earth's horizon.

trol and acquisition; and pointing and tracking technologies. In this section we will review significant portions of each DEW technology program.

Before we delve into the actual weapons concepts, however, it will be helpful if we first understand the way in which lasers work. The name laser is really an acronym for Light Amplification by Stimulated Emission of Radiation. Until about 25 years ago, the idea of a laser was pure fantasy—the kind of stuff from which good science fiction was made.

As it happens, there was scientific fact to back up the all-powerful rays of light in science fiction. Atoms and molecules can absorb and store, for a short time, certain amounts of energy. A wave of light energy can be absorbed by an atom; once done, that atom is 'raised' to an excited state. Once in that excited state, the atom may then radiate the light energy. The freed light energy can then be absorbed by another atom. However, if an already excited atom is stimulated to radiate its stored energy by another wave of light, the suddenly released radiation will strengthen the second wave of light. This fact of physics is, simply put, the basis for the laser.

The key to harnessing the almost mythical beam of light was to find a way first to excite a group of atoms and then to stimulate them to give up their stored energy simultaneously. The difficulty in this was the fact that if there are more un-

excited atoms present in a given area than there are excited atoms, the absorption of light waves will occur significantly more frequently than will radiation. A second problem in producing a laser was the speed with which atoms absorb and then release their energy (in about a millionth of a second).

The 1957 solution to the problem was eloquent. Imagine a column shaped in the form of a test tube. At one end of the test tube imagine a mirror, and at the other end imagine a similar mirror but with a small hole in the middle. Now encircle the test tube with a powerful strobe light and (with your imagination again) fill the test tube with atoms. You now have the basics of a laser. To create the beam of laser light you must simply begin to flash the strobe and the reaction begins. The atoms are excited by the initial strobe pulse and then stimulated to release their energy by subsequent pulses. Light also bounces off the mirrors at either end of our test tube. The reaction continues (strobe pulses, light being absorbed by atoms, light being released by atoms stimulated by other light waves, light bounding off the mirrors further strengthening the intensity, etc) until at some point light escapes from the small hole in the mirror—and we have our laser beam.

This beam of light is unlike most because it is highly directional. Only the waves that travel along the length of our test tube make it through the hole in the mirror. Further, because

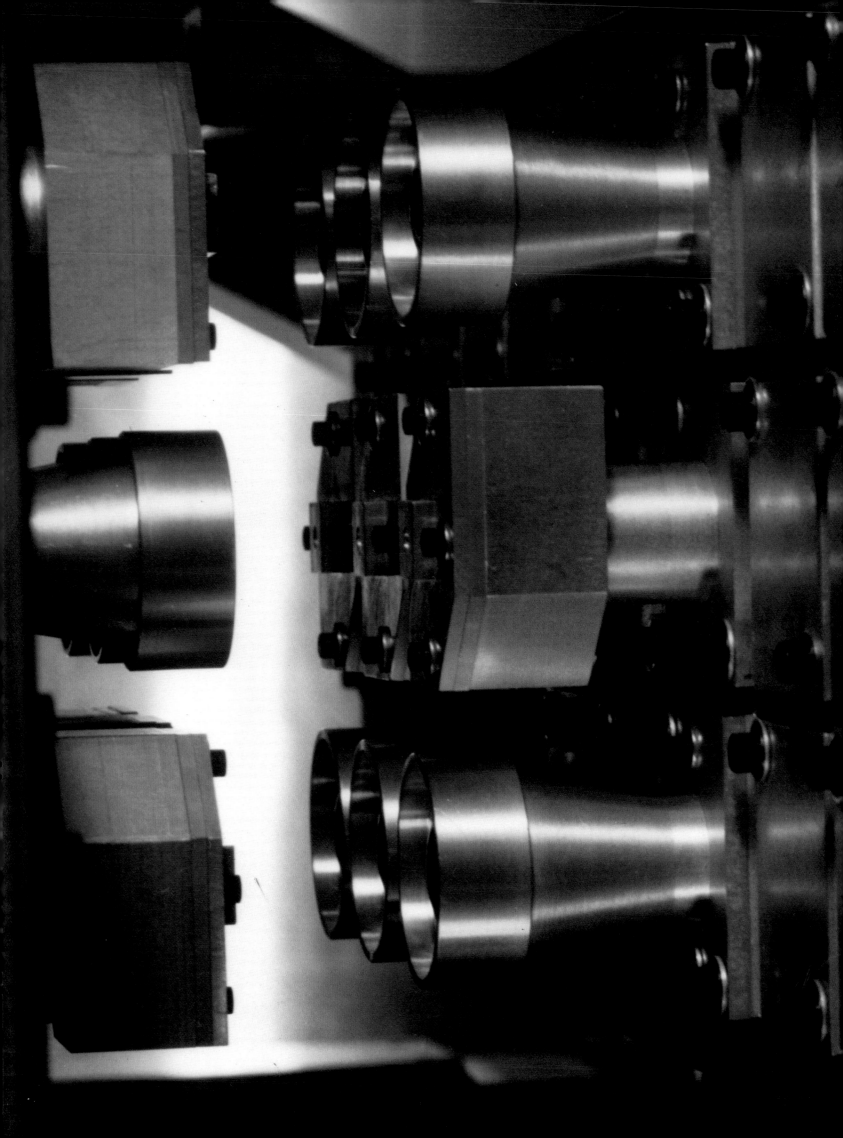

of the way atoms are forced to give up their stored energy, the light produced by a laser is of a single color (monochromatic) and, because all of the individual atoms are stimulated to give up their stored energy at the same time, the light wave which is produced between the mirrors is said to be coherent—that is, of one specific wave length. The light from a laser is also an amplification of the original light wave which began the laser reaction. This is not only because the atoms are stimulated to radiate light faster than they would have on their own, but also because the light emitted tends to amplify the light which originally stimulated the atoms. By definition, we may say that the light produced by lasers is direction-specific, monochromatic, coherent and extremely powerful.

The early lasers produced several thousand watts of power and had a power density on the order of 10 thousand watts per one-third of a square inch. Hard to believe as it is, this power density is greater than the intensity of light at the surface of our sun. More importantly, the beam of light could be focused with the aid of a lens, to produce a power density of millions of watts per one-third of a square inch.

It is clear why lasers were interesting for potential military applications. Because an intense beam of light produces such enormous power on a very small area, the beam can quite literally burn a hole through an otherwise strong material. For example, the skin of a Soviet SS-18 ICBM is not much thicker than about six pages of this book. Clearly, it would not take a significant amount of energy to rupture its shell and then ignite the thousands of gallons of fuel in the interior. Missiles have such thin walls simply out of weight con-

Left: The power source and the cone-shaped focusing optics of this Lockheed-designed laser weapon are kept in alignment by the laser's beam itself and by magnetism. The MIRACL chemical laser (*below*) at White Sands' testing facility — acronymed for its makers' hopes?

sideration; they cannot afford to carry the unusable dead weight of a heavier skin. Another weak spot in the missile design is the electronics carried on board. Such electronics are used for guidance of the missile and warheads as well as for warhead detonation. A well-placed laser 'shot' could easily disrupt these on board electronics. The wounded missile would fall back to earth (if it does not explode first).

The difficulty with lasers had been that the equipment which produced them was large. More importantly, even if there were a way to apply their power for military application, there was still a problem of how to aim the beam. Remember, we have already said that the beam from a laser is highly directional. In order to destroy a missile which was even a few hundred miles away, the beam would have to hit the target. Military planners continued to study laser technology, waiting for advancements in the field.

In the 30 years since the first laser, the technology has improved greatly. We now have optically pumped lasers, gas discharge lasers, semiconductor diode lasers, chemical lasers and free-electron lasers—to name only a few. The dramatic advances in laser science have brought laser weaponry applicability to the forefront. The beam weapon of science fiction is nearing reality. Two of these laser types have gained the interest of Strategic Defense Initiative planners. These are the chemical laser and the free-electron laser.

The chemical laser has long been a promising technology for defense planners. Until recently the highest energy single-beam laser in the world was a chemical laser designed and built for the Navy by TRW. The Mid-Infrared Advanced Chemical Laser (MIRACL) at the High Energy Laser Systems Test Facility (HELSTF) of White Sands Missile Range was originally designed to explore the utility of a high energy laser for the close-in air defense of ships. A deuterium-flouride chemical laser, MIRACL was designed to pro-

120

Above, below right and opposite—sequentially: This Laser Lethality Test was conducted at the White Sands Missile Base on 6 September 1985. The MIRACL deuterium-fluorine chemical laser, the most powerful laser outside the USSR, destroyed the test object—a Titan I missile body, sans fuel but stressed to simulate operating conditions.

duce about two megawatts of powerful light, having produced an output of 2.2 megawatts at a wavelength of about 3.8 microns. The tests of MIRACL proved that it was possible to focus a laser beam on a small spot at long range. This ability is obviously a prerequisite for any useful defense system laser weapons application. The MIRACL laser program will be integrated into an experimental device for groundbased lethality testing against targets at White Sands Missile Range. Ground experiments will be conducted to see if scientists can efficiently integrate a laser and a beam director. Eventually, MIRACL will likely be used to shoot down sounding rockets in carefully controlled tests. Even though this will be an operational laser system in a sense, it will not be in any violation of the 1972 ABM Treaty. The power, optics and laser frequency are not compatible for beam propagation in the atmosphere.

Because of the success of MIRACL experiments, TRW has been selected to build a 'next-generation' chemical laser. This new laser, called Alpha, will be a groundbased laser device designed to demonstrate the feasibility of high power infrared chemical lasers for spacebased applications. The Alpha is a large cylindrical laser device which may be a compact way to provide a spacebased infrared laser option. Alpha will be a hydrogen-fluorine laser designed to emit energy at a wave length of 2.7 microns. The initial power of this equipment is intended to be on the order of two megawatts. However, with the addition of generators, it is expected that peak power will be on the order of about ten megawatts. The real test of Alpha will be in its range and power levels. This system's primary purpose is to investigate

the feasibility of building laser systems with an output as high as 25 megawatts—large enough to be used as a weapon.

Chemical lasers operate under the same basic principles as the basic laser device described earlier. However, the atoms used to store and release energy in their laser systems are volatile (in other words, easily excitable) gases such as hydrogen and fluorine. In these lasers, chemicals are forced into a reaction chamber where they react violently. The light emitted from the excited electrons is collected and concentrated by mirrors and then emerges as a laser beam. This sort of laser has been under study since the 1970s.

Because of its relative compactness, as compared to other types of lasers, the SDI investigation of chemical lasers is for use in the spacebased laser concept. This idea envisions self-contained laser battle stations which are modular in form. Modularity would allow the individual battle stations to be assembled into more powerful weapons (by combining the beams) if the threat against the defensive system were to grow. These battle stations would be deployed in orbits which would ensure that the required number of weapons are available to engage ballistic missile launches wherever they occur. The current concept envisions that spacebased lasers would be able to engage ballistic missiles launched from anywhere on earth—including ocean areas and Western Europe (shorter-range ballistic missiles).

At left is a conception of the Lockheed-designed USAF Alpha, projected to be a cylindrical, high power spacebased SDI directed energy weapon. *Below* is a view 'across the tube' of the eerie blue light of Los Alamos National Labs' Krypton Fluoride (KRF) laser.

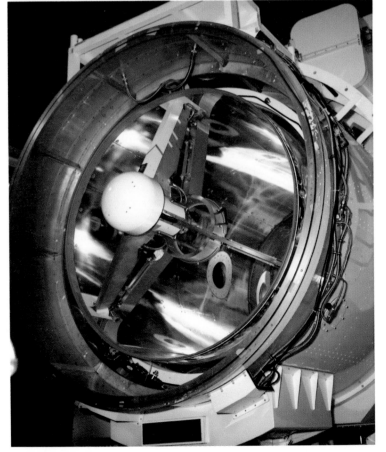

Opposite page: The US Navy's Hughes Aircraft-manufactured High Energy Laser Beam Director (HEL). *Immediate left:* This is a closeup of the HEL's mirror arrangement. *Above:* The TRW Defense and Space Systems Group laser, built for use with the HEL (*in mirror*).

This system of orbiting spacebased laser battle stations could play other significant roles in the defensive system. It would certainly be capable of engaging threats and destroying postboost vehicles before their reentry vehicles are deployed. Spacebased lasers could be called upon to destroy reentry vehicles and decoys in the midcourse phase. They could also defend other spacebased assets of the United States. Finally, the lasers could defend against some airborne threats. Since the laser beams of some lasers could penetrate into the atmosphere (down to the cloud tops), these lasers may be able to defend against some aircraft, cruise missiles and perhaps, even against tactical ballistic missiles.

The key to a successful laser weapon for defensive applications is the frequency of its electromagnetic radiation: the higher the frequency, the more powerful the beam. Remembering back to high school science, the electromagnetic spectrum spans a broad range of frequencies or wavelengths. These begin at the longest wavelength (the lowest frequency) radio waves and proceed through familiar areas such as broadcast waves (television), short wave, infrared, visible light, ultraviolet, X-rays, gamma rays and at the high end of the frequency spectrum (short wave length), cosmic rays.

In a laser, the beam of light is propagated in the infrared part of the electromagnetic spectrum. The task of scientists is

to increase the frequency of the beam (shorten the wavelength). Chemical lasers have produced powerful beams. However, the goal is to improve and produce a beam which is in the high infrared range—very close to the visible light range. More specifically, the goal for laser scientists is a beam with a wavelength of about one micron. Thus far, chemical lasers, while very powerful, have not been shown to be able to produce the desired power.

Recently, free-electron lasers have taken the forefront as the most promising technology for defense applications. This particular type of laser device has shown much promise in attaining the power objectives of SDI planners.

Free-electron lasers were little more than laboratory curiosities a few years ago. Given their success to date, these lasers could prove capable of producing power in the range of billions to trillions of watts.

To generate the laser beam, a free-electron laser must first have a stream of energetic electrons moving at a velocity which is near the speed of light. This requires accelerators similar to those developed more than 25 years ago for research in the field of nuclear physics. An accelerator is simply a long series of magnets (or magnetic fields) which may be turned on and off to attract an electron. As the electron moves, nearby magnets are turned off and those farther away are turned on. Thus, the electron is irresistibly drawn

forward through the accelerator. The faster the magnets are turned on and off, the faster the electron travels until the electron is near the speed of light (a 'relativistic electron').

The stream of relativistic electrons is then directed into another structure called a 'wiggler,' or undulator, which also has magnets. This time the magnets are placed in a fashion in which their poles are set to alternate (the first magnet has its positive pole next to the following magnet's negative pole, followed by another positive pole and so on).

When the stream of electrons travels over these alternating magnets, they are attracted by only one pole. Since the attracting pole is alternatingly at opposite ends of the next magnet, the relativistic electrons 'wiggle' transversely from the direction of the stream. This side-to-side movement forces the electrons to lose energy in the form of photons. These photons (which are very small increments of light) combine to become coherent laser light.

There are two different approaches to free-electron laser design. These approaches involve different methods for accelerating the beam of electrons. These two approaches are the Radio Frequency Linear Accelerator and the Induction Linear Accelerator. In the first method, the electrons are accelerated by means of microwave energy as the guide to control the stream of electrons through the wiggler. This method produces pulses of light, each lasting about twenty trillionths

Above and above left: These are views of Los Alamos National Laboratories' (LANL) Radio Frequency Linear Accelerator which was used in LANL's free electron laser experiment, which produced a very high power microwave beam. *At right:* UC Berkeley's 'wiggler' magnet produces coherent microwaves from high-current electron beams.

of a second. The average power of a radio frequency accelerated free-electron laser depends upon the density of the pulses within a packet (a group of pulses) and the repetition at which the packets are generated. The lethality of this type of laser is similar to a continuous-wave chemical laser.

The second method of producing the free-electron laser is to use a laser beam of modest power to start the reaction. The induction system then is basically a laser amplifier which adds energy to the laser beam as it passes through the wiggler with the electrons. The induction free-electron laser produces a very pronounced pulse of extremely high intensity. Indeed, the intensity of the beam is such that it is necessary to diffuse it somewhat before exposing it to mirrors (which it would otherwise destroy).

Free-electron lasers have three major advantages over their chemical laser counterparts. First, they are extremely powerful. Second, they have been shown to be much more efficient than chemical lasers. Finally, the purity of the beam, in terms of unwanted, spurious wave lengths, is superior to those so far generated by chemical lasers.

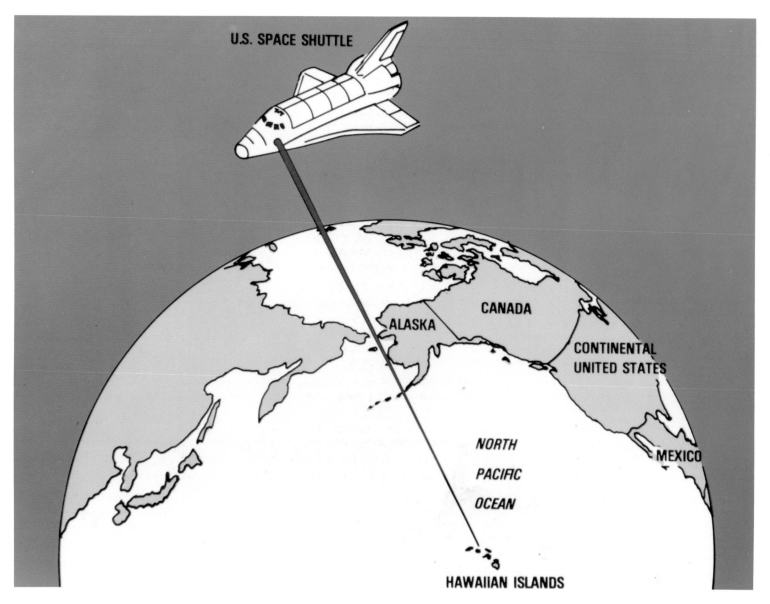

U.S. SPACE SHUTTLE

ALASKA

CANADA

CONTINENTAL UNITED STATES

NORTH PACIFIC OCEAN

MEXICO

HAWAIIAN ISLANDS

The High-Precision Tracking Experiment (*at top*) was conducted during Shuttle Orbiter *Discovery* flight 51-G on 17 June 1985. *Below:* The laser retroflector which was attached to *Discovery* 51-G. *Opposite, above and below:* A laser 'aiming' mirror; and LANL's KRF laser.

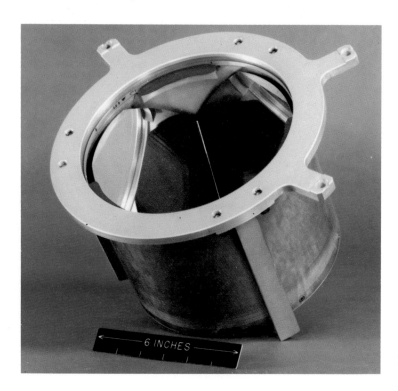

6 INCHES

The SDI investigation of free-electron lasers is at this point centered around a groundbased laser concept. This idea envisions several ground sites equipped with laser beam generators, target acquisition, tracking, pointing and (some sort of) beam control apparatus. Each station would be capable of generating a beam through the atmosphere to a relay mirror in outer space. These relay mirrors would collect and then redirect the beam to local launch area mission mirrors (also called fighting mirrors). The mission mirrors would collect the beam from the relay, acquire and track a threat target, and aim and focus the beam at the target. Beyond the technical problem of producing the laser beam, there is the difficulty of aiming it. The energy from a groundbased laser use for defense applications will need to travel quite a bit farther than will a beam from a spacebased battle station. Given a groundbased laser system with a relay mirror in geosynchronous orbit plus mission mirrors, a beam of energy could travel on the order of 60,000 miles before contacting its intended target. On the other hand, the energy from a spacebased laser battle station will need to travel only a few thousand miles.

To bring the aiming problem into perspective, hitting a target from a spacebased laser would be like hitting a baseball in New York with an arrow fired from Los Angeles. If a groundbased concept is applied, the arrow fired from Los Angeles would have to ricochet off a mountain in Alaska before speeding toward the target in New York.

Whether aimed directly or relayed through the use of mirrors, the aiming of a laser may well be easier than tracking the target. To be effective, a laser beam must dwell on a point on the target long enough to burn through and damage the target. Even though the laser beam travels at the speed of light, the movement of the target requires that the laser 'track' (that is, move with) the target in order for the beam to be able to dwell on one specific spot. The accuracy required is expressed in terms of microradians. A radian is the angular movement of a target over a specific period of time—a movement that the tracking system must match for the laser beam to dwell. Notice that the track accuracy is in *micro*radians— that is, in *millionths* of a radian.

Because there are so many questions in the area of aiming and tracking of lasers, the SDIO will fund a Space Acquisition, Tracking and Pointing (SATP) experiment to demonstrate technologies required for this important aspect of defense research.

If the free-electron laser concept moves ahead, an operational induction system for defense purposes might consist of six widely separated 'laser farms.' Each farm would possibly contain six or more of the high power free-electron laser systems. Each laser will be capable of generating hundreds of megawatts of average power at a near-infrared wavelength of about one micron.

Two major difficulties of the induction free-electron laser system are the intensity of its beam and the size of the facility needed to produce a usable beam. As already mentioned, the very intense power of these lasers is such that the beam must be diffused somewhat before it can be pointed at a mirror. At the very high power levels required for defense system applications, it will likely be necessary to force the beam first through a vacuum chamber to allow it to expand to a larger diameter, thereby reducing power density.

The size of the induction free-electron laser system is a 'given' application at this time. The accelerator which is used to whip the electrons to nearly the speed of light will be about a mile in length—this includes the electron accelerator and the 'wiggler'—and to allow for beam expansion, a two and one-half mile vacuum tube is also necessary. Overall, each laser farm will need a space approximately four miles long and one mile in width.

Although the free-electron laser technology shows much promise for future defense applications, there are at least five significant challenges which must be overcome during the next few years. First is the problem of optics. Devising optical systems to relay and focus the beams, without their being damaged at the same time, will be one of the most difficult problems to overcome. The SDIO will fund the High Brightness Relay (HIBREL) project consisting of a series of experiments to demonstrate the feasibility of relay mirrors in space for groundbased lasers. Also worthy of mention here is the Large Optics Demonstration Experiment (LODE) which will produce a 13-foot optical system designed to establish the feasibility of producing larger, high quality beam control devices.

Beam control optics present a fascinating problem for scientists. Mirrors must be capable of focusing sufficient energy on a target to cause irreparable damage, while at the same time not being themselves destroyed by that same energy pulse. With this in mind, the construction of mirrors will be a formidable task. The surface precision—evenness and reflectivity—will need to be of a very high quality. It is likely that these several, comparatively smaller mirrors will

be easier to construct than one large one. The problem of mirror quality does not end once the equipment is on station in space. Planners can look forward to the problem of contamination in space. Long exposure in orbit will result in a never-ending series of collisions with molecules and small particles. Over time, these collisions will pit the surface of the mirrors. This sort of damage could eventually lead to the failure of the mirrors when they are stressed by a powerful surge of laser energy.

Another mirror-related problem is one of 'spillover.' When the laser beam is reflected by a mirror, some of the light in the beam spills over the edge of the mirror into the surrounding space. This spillover tends to spoil the laser's perfection, because parts of the beam begin to travel at an angle to the original beam's direction. In short the beam is no longer highly directional (which is one of the characteristics of a laser's power). This spillover causes the laser beam to spread as it travels—resulting in less intensity at the focus point on the target.

The second problem is one known as 'stimulated Ramon scattering.' This effect results from absorption of laser beam energy by molecules in the atmosphere. Like atoms absorbing light, these molecules are stimulated by the absorption of laser energy which causes them to spontaneously radiate new photons which are at a wavelength different than that of the original beam. The effect of this is the divergence of the beam, which in turn reduces power density at the target. Because of the intense power of the free-electron laser, this Ramon scattering is a potentially serious problem.

The third problem with groundbased laser systems is one known as thermal 'blooming.' The energy of a laser (particularly a laser of defense system intensity) affects more than just the target at which it is aimed. The beam tends to heat the air through which it passes. This heating of the environment immediately adjacent to the beam has been shown to defocus the beam, which in turn reduces power density at the target.

Another phenomenon of laser beam interaction with the atmosphere is one of ionization (electrical breakdown of the air). This ionization can generate plasmas which can seriously attenuate or block the passage of the beam. Plasma is a curious phenomenon. At extremely high temperatures, matter can become plasma—which is a gas that has become so hot electrons normally bonded to atoms are stripped away, resulting in the formation of a field or cloud of ions with positive and negative charges.

The final challenge for scientists in developing a groundbased laser defense system is good old-fashioned atmospheric turbulence. Atmospheric fluctuation can disturb the coherence of a laser beam. This disruption causes problems when trying to focus the beam. This is one problem which is well on its way to being solved. Through a technique known as adaptive optics, a low power laser beam is transmitted to a spacebased sensor which is close to a fighting mirror. The spacebased sensor measures the amount of distortion in the low power beam, and 'pre-distorts' the weapon laser to work *with* the effects of the atmospheric distortion, which is then actually contributing to the production of a beam of the desired intensity.

The promise of the free-electron laser system is such that SDIO may develop a half scale version of the facility required. This prototype would be developed over the next two years by the Lawrence Livermore National Laboratory. As proposed, the test system would initially use the Livermore Advanced Technology Accelerator with a 16-foot long wiggler. This wiggler will eventually be enlarged to a total length of 82 feet. In addition to increasing the power of the laser beam, scientists will need to design a fast and reliable switching system for the wiggler in order to speed up the electron stream. Once this is done, they will need to extract the energy very quickly: the energy burst of electrons usually occurs in about 60 billionths of a second.

The problem of using a laser to shoot at a target on the other side of the world can be brought home using a simple set of examples. Imagine trying to focus a standard 100 watt light bulb through the use of a magnifying glass. The light could be narrowed into a fairly bright spot of about one-eighth to one-quarter of an inch in diameter. Although the light would be bright it would not be powerful enough to burn through anything. If, on the other hand, we used a magnifying glass to focus a 100 watt laser, the spot of focused light would be far narrower, less than one one-hundredth of an inch in diameter. The intense light produced from this focused 100 watt laser is powerful enough to cut through steel as much as one-eighth of an inch thick! As we move toward using lasers for weapons systems, the power must be increased to compensate for the beam's spreading as it travels across the thousands of miles of space toward its target. Depending on the distance traveled, a laser beam may have spread to a degree where it might be one foot in diameter as it 'rests' on the target. This relative lack of focus, as compared to the one one-hundredth of an inch discussed above, results in the need for a significant increase in focus in order to produce the desired damage results on the target. Keeping things in perspective, if an ordinary light has been projected across the same distance, the light at the focus point would be several miles in diameter.

One final laser type is being explored by the SDIO. This is the 'eximer' laser device and, although not quite so promising as the free-electron laser, it deserves a brief mention here.

Above opposite: The powerful KRF laser, aka 'Aurora.' *Below:* This artist's conception of a high power free-electron laser test facility indicates the system's major components—linear electron accelerator, master oscillator and laser amplifier, or 'wiggler.'

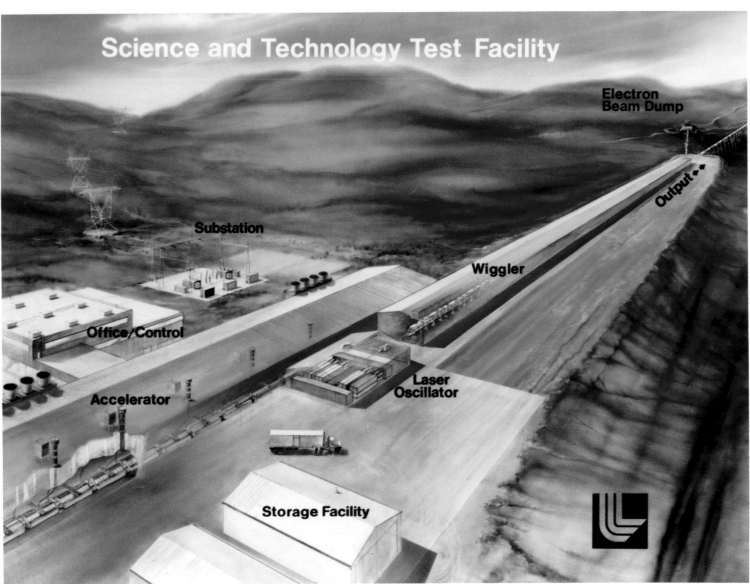

The eximer laser derives its name from the term 'excited dimer.' A dimer is a molecule which is made of an inert gas such as krypton, and a halogen such as fluorine. An inert gas does not readily combine with other atoms. In order to form a dimer, an electric current must be passed through a mixture of inert and halogen gases. This electric current causes an excited state. When this unstable molecule (a dimer) decays, it emits a photon of light in the range between visible and ultraviolet on the electromagnetic spectrum. This process results in a chain reaction of decaying dimers, which eventually gives rise to a coherent laser beam. When the majority of eximer molecules decay into separate atoms, no new photons will be produced and the laser reaction ends. The reaction is exceptionally quick, about one-millionth of a second for the laser pulse—brief, but very intense and powerful.

Overall, eximer lasers are less efficient than chemical or free-electron lasers in terms of energy conversion. The possible advantage of eximer lasers is that arrays of the devices can be easily combined to produce one very powerful beam. A

The Sperry Corporation spacebased laser envisioned *above* could intercept ICBMs in their boost phase, before warhead deployment, and may be useful against interatmospheric weaponry as well. *Right:* Lasers this size may soon be science 'fact.'

significant SDI project is the Eximer Repetitively Pulsed Laser Device (EMRLD). The goal of this project is to produce a laser in the megawatt power range before 1990.

Although there are still challenges to overcome, laser technology promises to be a key to the defense system of the future. Given the relative power density capabilities of the systems available, it seems likely that the first systems for defense applications will be groundbased and will utilize spacebased mirrors to deflect a light beam toward its target. There is a role for spacebased laser battle stations but this will no doubt come after much improvement in chemical or eximer laser technology, or after the development of a compact free-electron type laser system. No matter what the system, the science fiction 'ray guns' of just a few years ago could soon be a reality.

A GENUINE,
Official

BUCK ROGERS ROCKET PISTOL
that retails for 20¢

Brand New!

THINK THIS OVER!!

★ A brand new *genuine* Buck Rogers Rocket Pistol . . . 7½ inches long.

★ Has *every* feature found on the original Rocket Pistol—the toy sensation of 1934.

★ Packed in the same famous display carton that pulled such tremendous sales for the original Rocket Pistol.

★ New low price opens up a huge NEW market for you!

★ Nationally advertised—naturally—like everything DAISY builds—your guarantee of *100% SALABILITY.*

Ready for delivery about February 1st. All orders will be filled in the order they're received. We will gladly furnish you additional information and prices.

and of course

IT'S A DAISY

DAISY MANUFACTURING COMPANY, PLYMOUTH, MICHIGAN

There are three other SDI research efforts underway which also produce beams of destructive energy. These are neutral particle beams, charged particle beams and so-called X ray lasers. Each of these concepts is an interesting SDI research efforts and is worthy of some consideration.

The neutral particle beam is a spacebased weapons concept utilizing accelerated negative ions as the disruptive energy force. The neutral particle beam weapons envisioned would be configured much like the spacebased lasers. A series of these weapons would be placed in an orbital network which would be capable of engaging ballistic missile boosters and postboost vehicles as their launch trajectories lift them out of the atmosphere.

A particle beam weapon can disable a missile without actually destroying it. The beam of charged particles would not burn a hole in the skin of a missile as would a laser beam. Instead, the particle beam would easily pass through the skin of a vehicle and disrupt the electronic devices on board. Neutral particle beams are effective at altitudes of about 90 miles. More importantly, neutral particle beams offer the promise of efficient boostphase destructive force. SDI planners are definitely interested in the fact that particle beam weapons have an unlimited stream of energy. Because of this (and the fact that the beams penetrate through the target), these weapons do not need to dwell on targets like lasers. Interestingly, much of our base knowledge regarding neutral particle beams comes from Russia. Soviet scientists have been studying this area of science for some time. Indeed, their research literature included extensive discussions about their research efforts. Apparently they became aware of the potential sensitivity of the research, and 10 years ago they suddenly stopped reporting on the subject.

The method of creating a beam such as this is familiar to us as it will sound similar to our free-electron laser system. Particle beam weapons would use an accelerator to speed up a stream of negative ions to a velocity near the speed of light. As with the accelerators discussed earlier, these particles are driven down the length of the accelerator by pulsing electromagnetic fields. The negative ions are drawn even faster by the speed of on-off switching of the electromagnetic fields. Near the end of the accelerator a final series of magnets 'point' the particle beam at the target. Prior to leaving the weapon, though, one final step is required: the ions are stripped of their negative charge. This is a key step in the process; if the negative charge were not taken away, the negative ions in the beam would repel one another and the beam would become diffused. Further, negative ions in the beam could be attracted to the magnetic field of Earth, and as a result would be deflected from their intended target.

Although intended as a weapon, the spacebased particle beam stations could also provide a sensor function for the defense system during the postboost and midcourse phases of a missile trajectory. It appears that when an object is 'hit' by a particle beam, it emits gamma rays and neutrons. The

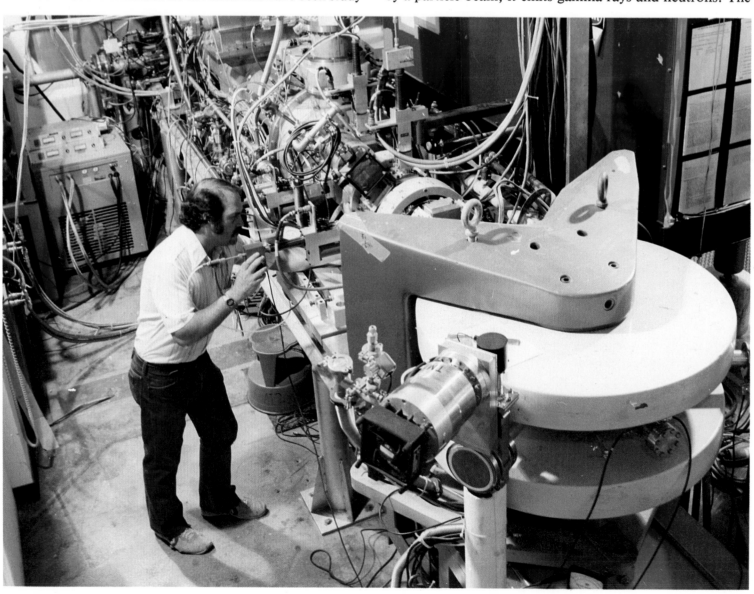

At left, a technician inspects equipment that is part of Los Alamos National Laboratories' neutral particle beam weapon experiment. *Above:* In this conception, a spacebased neutral particle beam 'gun' destroys *at least a few* hostile ICBMs.

gamma rays and neutrons released seem to be in proportion to the size and mass of the object. With this in mind, these emissions could be used to discriminate between lightweight decoys and heavier reentry vehicles.

Particle beam technology could also provide the same destruction punch as lasers. Depending upon what sort of particles are used (there are many choices: electrons, protons, hydrogen atoms, etc), the beam can have a physical impact as well as an electrical one. This physical impact would be quite destructive because of the near-lightspeed velocity of the beam. It could be that the particle beams of the future will have the capability of either physically destroying a target or disabling it by way of electronic disruption.

There is no doubt that the particle beam technology weapons concept can be represented in some future version of a defense system. Experimentation in this technology is proceeding quite successfully. Recently, scientists developed and successfully tested the radio-frequency quadruple pre-accelerator. This device both accelerates and bunches a charged ion beam. This development is considered a major improvement in particle beam technology. Experiments have also produced an ion beam with qualities superior to SDI design goals. Also, scientists have demonstrated a method for precision aiming of a neutral beam. Testing will continue—the Neutral Particle Beam Technology Integration experiment is designed to investigate the technologies needed to perform midcourse discrimination or to detect nuclear

material. This experiment will be conducted in space at low power levels and use nearby co-orbital instrumented targets. In compliance with the 1972 ABM Treaty, the device will not be capable of autonomously acquiring or tracking ballistic missile targets. The Neutral Particle Beam (NPB) Midcourse Discrimination Technology experiment will eventually require the use of the space shuttle.

While an actual particle beam weapon is still years off, the technology holds such promise that the Strategic Defense Initiative Organization has funded a dedicated particle beam test bed at the Brookhaven National Laboratory. SDI planners seem confident that neutral particle beams have practical applications for both sensor and weapons missions in the strategic defense system.

In concept, charged particle beams are a bit more difficult to handle. Charged particles such as electrons are attracted by the magnetic field of Earth. This attraction distorts the beam and makes targeting impossible. Complicating this, the charged particles tend to repel one another—causing the beam to swell and lose power intensity. Still, some recent advances give hope that charged particle beams could be used.

It seems that a laser can be used effectively to clear a channel in the Earth's magnetic field for the beam of charged particles. Since there is virtually no magnetic field in the cleared channel, the electrons travel in a straight line: the laser beams tend to knock electrons off some of the atoms in the air, and these electrons move in a spiraling path along the direction of the laser beam as a result of the force of the laser strike (and the force exerted by the Earth's magnetic field). The spiraling electrons generate a magnetic field of their own but—most important—this field tends to cancel out the ef-

fect of the Earth's field. We have already noted that similarly charged particles tend to repel one another and the beam spreads, but scientists have come up with an interesting fact—when a number of negatively-charged electrons are knocked out of the channel by a laser, a net residue postive charge is left behind. Thus we have a spiraling series of negatively charged electrons surrounding a positive field. When a flow of electrons is directed down the channel toward a target, the spiraling electrons hold a positive field within, and the positive field tends to help compress the stream of negatively-charged electron bullets. It is *almost* like rolling marbles down a pipe.

Charged particle weapons are still a long way off. However, scientists are making tremendous progress in this fascinating area of physics.

We now come to X-ray laser. This laser is really a particle beam concept which is a 'one shot' weapon. An X-ray laser utilizes a very compact, highly organized and direction specific beam of X-rays to destroy a target. The only way known to generate an X-ray beam powerful enough to have a destructive force is to 'pump' the X-ray by means of a nuclear explosion.

The way this weapon would work is really quite simple. A low-yield nuclear bomb (on the order of one to about 20 kilotons of explosive force) is placed inside a spherically-shaped containment vessel. On the outside of the spherical container are tubes with a length of metal wire running from the container to the end of the tube.

To pump X-rays, the nuclear explosive is detonated. In the milliseconds before the spherical container, tubes and wire are disintegrated by the explosion, the nuclear burst creates X-rays which are conducted through the tubes by the metal wire and then out toward the target. Because of the nature of the explosion, the X-rays are in the form of a highly condensed 'pulse' of electromagnetic particles traveling at nearly the speed of light. The force of this pulse would be tremendous—and the target would be burned by the particles and crushed by the shock.

Since the technology for this X-ray laser is available now, a weapon of this sort could be the first element of a strategic defense network. However, there are three key points which must be considered before a deployment decision is made. First: since this is a one-shot device, how can this weapon be used to shoot down more than one offensive missile threat? One can imagine a device looking very much like a mechanical porcupine—a ball studded with movable tubes. Each tube would be moved independently to track a particular target until the ball is detonated and hundreds of X-ray pulses speed toward their mark. The aiming is the crucial element. To track and aim more than a few tubes prior to detonation will require some fairly sophisticated systems. Obviously, since the entire device will disintegrate after the first shot, it is necessary to keep the cost of the system to a minimum.

The second element to be considered is how to deploy such a weapon. If these were set as orbital weapons platforms now, they would be in clear violation of the 1972 ABM Treaty. With this in mind, should a deployment decision be made, these devices would likely be 'pop-up' weapons: at notification of an offensive launch threat, these devices would be launched into a position which offered the optimum intercept angle. Because they could be launched only after the launch of a threat, it is not reasonable to believe that they could intercept missiles in the boost or postboost phases

Facing page: A technician fine tunes a segment of the Lawrence Livermore Labs' Advanced Test Accelerator. *Above* and *below* are views of fluid control valves at the White Sands Missile Range High Energy Laser Test Facility—home of the MIRACL laser, which puts out 2.2 megawatts of power at the 3.8 micron wavelength.

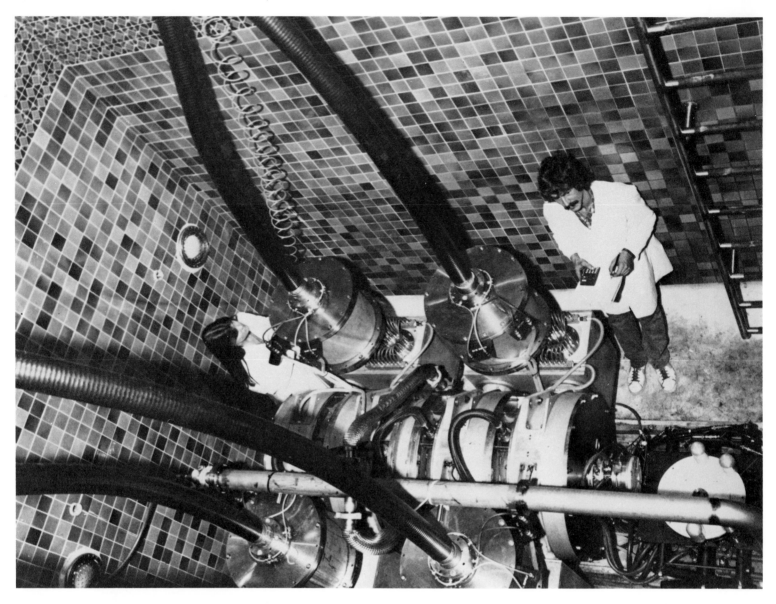

of flight. Rather, they would likely be used in midcourse—aimed at all suspected reentry vehicles.

If some sort of aiming device were perfected, these powerful weapons could be deployed as a pop-up defense and allow the United States to remain within the guidelines of the 1972 ABM Treaty. Proponents of an aggressive beam defense system have long advocated this approach.

There is one point that the proponents of X-ray lasers do not discuss very much, however. Although the aiming rods certainly direct an intense beam toward a target, there is also an electromagnetic pulse which emanates in all directions from the weapon—in effect, the weapon is indiscriminate in that it will disrupt any and all unprotected electronic equipment within the radius of the destructive pulse.

The third consideration which must be resolved before making a decision to deploy these X-ray laser weapons is one of consistency. The stated purpose of the Strategic Defense Intiative was to defend the United States and its allies from the threat of nuclear arms. We have a long history of living with nuclear weapons. The issue here is whether we should build nuclear arms in order to defend against nuclear arms. There are obvious pros and cons to the question. The decision to deploy this sort of weapon will not be easy to make.

The Strategic Defense Initiative Organization's investigation of directed-energy weapons is a multipurpose research effort. The goal of the research is to develop and advance directed-energy technology here in the United States. In

Physicists (*above*) check out Lawrence Livermore National Labs' two million electron volt 'High Brightness Test Stand' electron accelerator. The speculative sketch *at right* depicts a spacebased mirror system which directs Earthbased lasers onto high altitude targets.

terms of weapons research, the effort has a four part objective. The first objective is to advance energy beam generation technology. The goal is to produce various types of beams (laser, particle, etc) of specific quality and power intensity. The second objective is to be able to condition a beam in order to deliver it toward the target (that a beam is created does not automatically mean that it can be relayed toward a mark). If it is to be relayed via mirrors, the beam must be conditioned such that it will not destroy the mirrors or other optical devices. An efficient system will be one in which the optical element will be used more than once. Third—once in the vicinity of the target, the beam must be focused such that it can strike the target with sufficient intensity to disable it. The fourth objective of directed-energy research is to be able to aim and hold the beam on target for a sufficient duration so the the beam *can* disable it.

The SDI effort in directed energy will no doubt advance the science of wave and beam technology. It remains to be seen how soon this technology will be efficiently applied to a defense system architecture. It does seem more than likely though, that within the next 30 years science fiction will become reality, and we shall have the imagined 'ray guns' as key elements in our defensive arsenal.

THROWING ROCKS

8

Kinetic Energy Weapons may use electrical forces to fire a projectile, as is the case with the electromagnetic 'rail guns' which are being developed, or may themselves be the projectile which batters the target, like the HOE, shown *at left* lifting off and, *above right,* rising to its 'kill.'

Nearly every aspect of Strategic Defense Initiative effort is devoted to research and demonstration of the capability of our technology. This includes some of our more mature technologies. Kinetic energy weaponry has been around for centuries. Indeed, any weapon which is somehow propelled may be considered a kinetic energy device. Through the centuries we have hurled rocks and spears, shot arrows with bows, slung rocks with slingshots, fired bullets and rockets. At every stage of our existence on this planet there has been room for improvement of our weaponry, and today is not an exception.

Since the advent of the space age we have developed projectiles which could shoot down the weapons of an aggressor. For some time now, the defense against offensive weapons has seemed a futile effort. The advances in offensive capability have always surpassed the somewhat more humble efforts to plan and institute an effective defense. The SDI program has given new life to the idea of a strong, active defense. The kinetic energy weapons (KEW) of the future, when combined with the other elements of SDI, hold significant promise for the defense of the future. In fact, because

these KEW devices are relatively mature technologies, they would more than likely be used in an early deployment of a defense system.

Kinetic energy weapons destroy their targets by impact rather than by explosion. In fact, because these devices contain no explosives, they are commonly referred to as 'rocks.' 'Smart rocks' are those equipped with some sort of tracking or homing devices, while 'rocks' are simply solid projectiles. The goal of this Strategic Defense Initiative research program is to study ways to accurately direct relatively light projectiles at very high velocities in order to intercept ballistic missiles (or their warheads) during any phase of their flight.

Kinetic energy guided projectiles can be accelerated by chemically propelled boosters (rocket fuel for missiles and gun powder for bullets, for example), or perhaps in the future by hypervelocity electromagnetic methods. These SDI kinetic energy weapons rely chiefly on impact or nonnuclear explosives to destroy their nuclear targets. Obviously, the first requirement for a defense system is to locate and accurately track potential targets. Although we have discussed the problems in an earlier section, it is important to remember that tracking objects in space is not an easy task. Since the launch of the first artificial earth satellite, Sputnik I, there have been more than 15,000 objects placed into orbit around the earth. Although most of these devices are no

longer functional (many fell back to earth), we still monitor nearly 6000 orbiting objects, including live and dead satellites and spent rocket casings. To complicate matters further, there are more than 10,000 chunks of debris orbiting our planet. This debris is the remnant of space explosions over the years. If ever a conflict in space came about, the amount of space junk would increase tremendously, making tracking of real threats much more difficult and increasing the hazard of accidently running into one or more of these hidden 'rocks.' This clearly represents a serious risk for our future spacecraft, both manned and unmanned. A satellite in an even orbit at an altitude of 100 miles moves along at about 17,000 miles per hour. If the orbit were elliptical, the rate of speed would be roughly 23,000 miles per hour. Clearly, a collision with any object at such speeds could cause serious damage to any spacecraft. All of our future space planning must include a consideration for the challenges posed by space trash.

The SDI kinetic energy weapons research program is primarily centered around a three point objective: first, demonstration of a ground-launched kinetic energy kill vehicle (KKV) for endo- and exoatmospheric interception of nuclear warheads and missiles carrying those warheads; second, science and technology research in the area of spacebased, chemically-launched projectiles equipped with some sort of

Above: This is the tracking facility at Kwajalein Missile Range, which generated the photos *below, left to right* which follow the HOE experiment sequentially—from HOE's pre-collision rocket plume to discernable vehicle debris. *Opposite:* The HOE 'umbrella.'

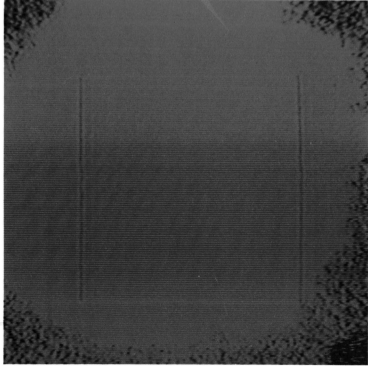

target homing device; and finally, research and development in the field of electromagnetically propelled projectiles for use as spacebased electromagnetic rail guns.

Perhaps one of the most publicized demonstrations of SDI technology was of a ground-launched kinetic energy kill vehicle. This demonstration was the Homing Overlay Experiment (HOE), in which an actual reentry vehicle midcourse intercept was conducted. A target missile was launched from Vandenberg Air Force Base in California, on a flight path which closely resembled the trajectory of an intercontinental ballistic missile. The course of the missile took it west over the Pacific. A nonnuclear interceptor was launched from the Kwajalein missile range in the central Pacific. For reference, Kwajalein is in the Marshall Island chain, approximately 6000 miles away from the launch site in California. While the drone ICBM was on its trajectory, the interceptor was accelerated to a speed of more than 20,000 miles per hour. When the radar at Kwajalein acquired the target, the interceptor was directed toward it and given final (automatic) control of the intercept. The HOE's upper stage (the homing and kill stage) included long wavelength infrared detection and homing techniques for in-flight guidance to the target. Prior to contact with the target, the interceptor unfurled a metal ribbed array structure with a diameter of about 15 feet. Because of the closure speed of the two objects (nearly 30,000 per hour) there was no need for an explosive device on the interceptor. When the two missiles made contact at an altitude of about 90 miles above the Pacific, they had a combined closure speed of about 5.5 miles per second (almost 20,000 miles per hour). When the two made contact, the force of the impact destroyed both missiles.

The intercept of the ICBM was quite significant for defense system planners. It showed that the technology was available to 'kill' offensive threats in the late boost through midcourse phases of a ballistic missile trajectory. The precision of the event was particularly impressive. Knocking out a missile at an altitude of something better than 100 miles is akin to 'shooting a bullet with a bullet.'

Another type of kinetic energy weapon is one that can strike an incoming warhead inside the earth's atmosphere.

Although accuracy is the prime objective for all SDI weaponry, these weapons must be reliable for they are the last layer of protection envisioned in the defense network. This vehicle, the High Endoatmospheric Defense Interceptor (HEDI) is envisioned to have an infrared guidance system and liquid rocket engines mounted on its sides for last-second lateral displacement towards the target. These vehicles are also envisioned to have a small radar homing device for target tracking. The overall project for this terminal phase system is named the Flexible Lightweight Agile Guided Experiment (FLAGE). The goal of FLAGE is to determine whether guidance accuracy, sufficient to achieve a nonnuclear kill within the atmosphere, can be attained.

Thus far, the FLAGE experiments have been promising. In the most extensive test to date, a simulated reentry vehicle was dropped from an aircraft at an altitude of 44,000 feet. A FLAGE missile intercepted the 'warhead' at an altitude of 12,000 feet and destroyed it. The interceptor, using a millimeter wave radar system, reached the warhead about seven seconds after launch. For the future, FLAGE technology developments (in both endo- and exoatmospheric kinetic kill vehicles) are needed in the areas of homing devices, maneuvering methods (lateral movement capability), boost propulsion, fire and guidance control.

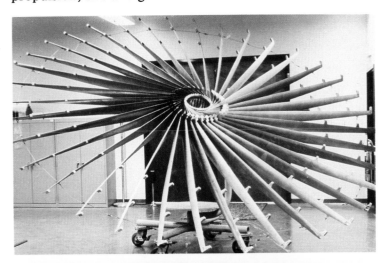

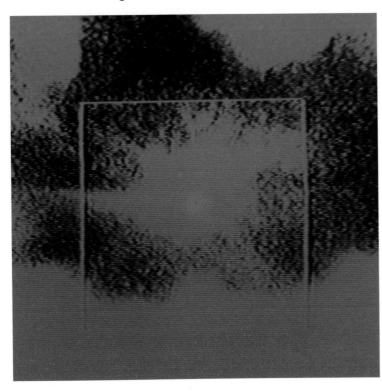

These are sequential photos of the successful 27 June 1986 FLAGE weapon test—a USN F-4 (*above*) carries the 'target'; the target deploys and FLAGE (*tip of white streak*) homes in (*below left and right*), and both the hypersonic FLAGE and its target destruct (*opposite*).

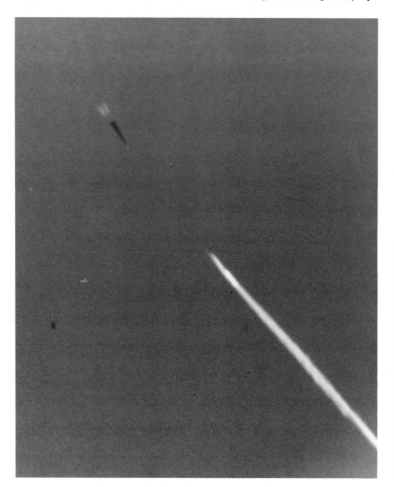

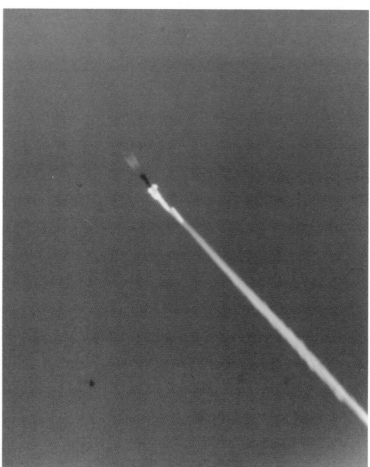

Projectile-firing rail guns: The CHECMATE Electromagnetic Launcher (*above left*) at Maxwell Laboratories, Inc in San Diego; another view (*above right*) of same; CHECMATE firing a .5 lb projectile (*below*) at a velocity of 7000 mph; and a closeup (*opposite*) of the operation.

Yet to be defined is how to approach the problem of space-based chemically-launched projectiles. It is likely that, once defined, the spacebased kinetic kill vehicle will include many of the elements of the Homing Overlay Experiment. The vehicle would likely be relatively small, because it would not need to carry the large amount of propellent needed to exit the atmosphere. Since such vehicles will be based in space, it is likely that they will be clustered in small groups; there would be little reason to put a one-shot weapon in orbit. One research program in this area is the Exoatmospheric Reentry Vehicle Interceptor Experiment (ERIS). This program will draw on many other research efforts, and will hopefully further develop the direct collision interception tactic demonstrated by the Homing Overlay Experiment.

The SDIO project list includes a Space-Based Kinetic Kill Vehicle (SBKKV) project. However, the objectives have yet to be specifically stated. The general purpose of the project is to establish the technology for chemically-propelled spacebased interceptors. This will be more of an exploration of options than a demonstration of technology. The project will not attempt to conduct a spacebased experiment (in other words, there will be no intercepts of ballistic missile targets). This lack of specific definition is probably due to the still technologically advanced nature of spacebased chemical rockets. Several ideas are on the drawing boards, however, and these are based in part on current interceptor technology. In one realistic design, the interceptor will use thrusters to approach a target and then simply explode. The explosion will send a cloud of flak fragments toward the target. The flight pattern of the interceptor would be varied depending

upon the target. In one scenario, the interceptor would be maneuvered into the same orbit as the target. This method takes up to several hours, however. A faster method would be to keep the interceptor in a (faster) low altitude orbit until it is beneath the track of the intended target. At a specific point the interceptor will use its speed advantage to pop up to the level of the target and home in for the kill.

Hypervelocity rail guns are, at least conceptually, an attractive alternative for a spacebased defense system. This is because of their envisioned ability to quickly 'shoot' at many targets. Also, because only the projectile leaves the gun, the gun can carry many projectiles.

Interestingly, a hypervelocity rail gun works very much like a nuclear accelerator. A metal pellet (the projectile) is attracted down a guide (the rail) of magnetic fields and accelerated by the rapid on-off switching of the various fields. The speeds attained by these small projectiles are dazzling. In one experiment a small particle was accelerated to a velocity of more than 24 miles per second (at that speed the projectile could circle our earth at the equator in something less than 20 minutes).

The SDI rail gun investigation, called the Compact High Energy Capicator Module Advanced Technology Experiment (CHECMATE), has been able to fire two projectiles per day. This represents a significant improvement over previous efforts which were only able to achieve about one shot per month. One of the major technical challenges of the rail gun experiments is the rapid firing of the gun. The challenge has to do with the rails. In order to rapidly accelerate the pellet, the rail must rapidly switch its magnetic fields on and

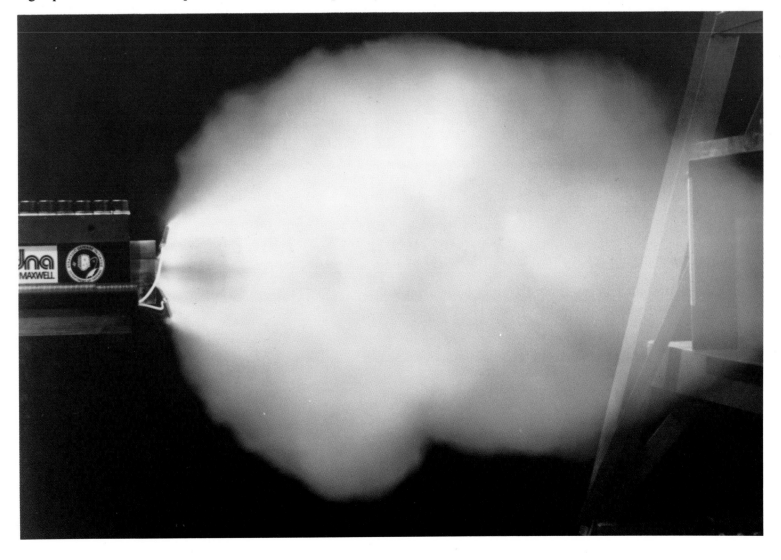

off. This extremely fast switching requires a tremendous current of electricity (almost one-half million amperes) to pass through the rails every time the gun is fired. In some experiments the rails had to be replaced after each firing.

Another challenge with the rail gun is the rapid acceleration of the projectile. At the speeds mentioned above, the acceleration stresses the pellet to pressures in excess of 100,000 times the normal force of gravity. In more popular terms, the acceleration of the pellet can be expressed in terms of 100,000 'Gs.' A 'G' is the acceleration of an object which is acted upon by gravity. If we drop a rock from a bridge, for instance, that rock will pick up speed at a rate of one G. As a passenger of a modern jetliner, you are pushed into your seat at takeoff by the one to two G acceleration. Imagine the six to nine G's felt by fighter pilots in today's performance aircraft. On the average, humans tend to black out at about 10 G's. Even with this limited view of G forces, it is easy to understand that the jolt of explosive acceleration in a rail gun could easily tear the bullet apart. In order to be effective, the bullet must be able to withstand the initial acceleration in order to get to the target. Further, if there ever were to be homing devices in larger rail gun projectiles, that projectile would need to be hardened to keep its shape, and the electronics inside it would need to be able to function after being stressed by the initial acceleration.

Experiments on hypervelocity rail gun technology will continue. The near-term goal is to fire 20 shots per week. Each shot is to accelerate an approximately one-quarter pound pellet to a velocity of about three miles per second (a little more than 11,000 miles per hour). The purpose of the research is to build an information base about rail guns so that SDI planners will know how to apply the technology to the proposed defense system.

In addition to being considered for destroying ballistic missile threats, rail guns are also being planned for service in space platform (sensor and battle station) defense. This potential role reflects defense planner expectations that the rail guns of the future will be capable of not only rapid fire, but also of multiple firings (on the order of tens to hundreds of shots).

For the near future, kinetic energy weapons technology offers the only currently available defense against the threat of offensive ballistic missiles. Deployment of these weapons (specifically devices such as HOE) could be accomplished rapidly should a need arise. As for spacebased chemical rockets and rail guns, the reality is still some years off. However, the overall pace of KKV research and development is certainly promising.

The complexities and challenges of SDI research will likely seem simple when compared to the analysis required to decide whether or not to develop a strategic defense system. The decision to press on with the effort, either with all or some of the components discussed thus far, must be based on three key factors: effectiveness—the system must be capable of effectively defending the assets of the United States and its allies; survivability—the defensive network must be able not only to survive the rigors of a space environment, but also to withstand the attack (either actual physical attack or disruptive countermeasures) of an aggressor; and affordability—the system cannot be burdensome in terms of either cost to deploy or cost to maintain.

Rapid-fire rail guns such as Boeing's Sagittar concept (*upper right*) are within the reach of the fast advancing SDI technology.

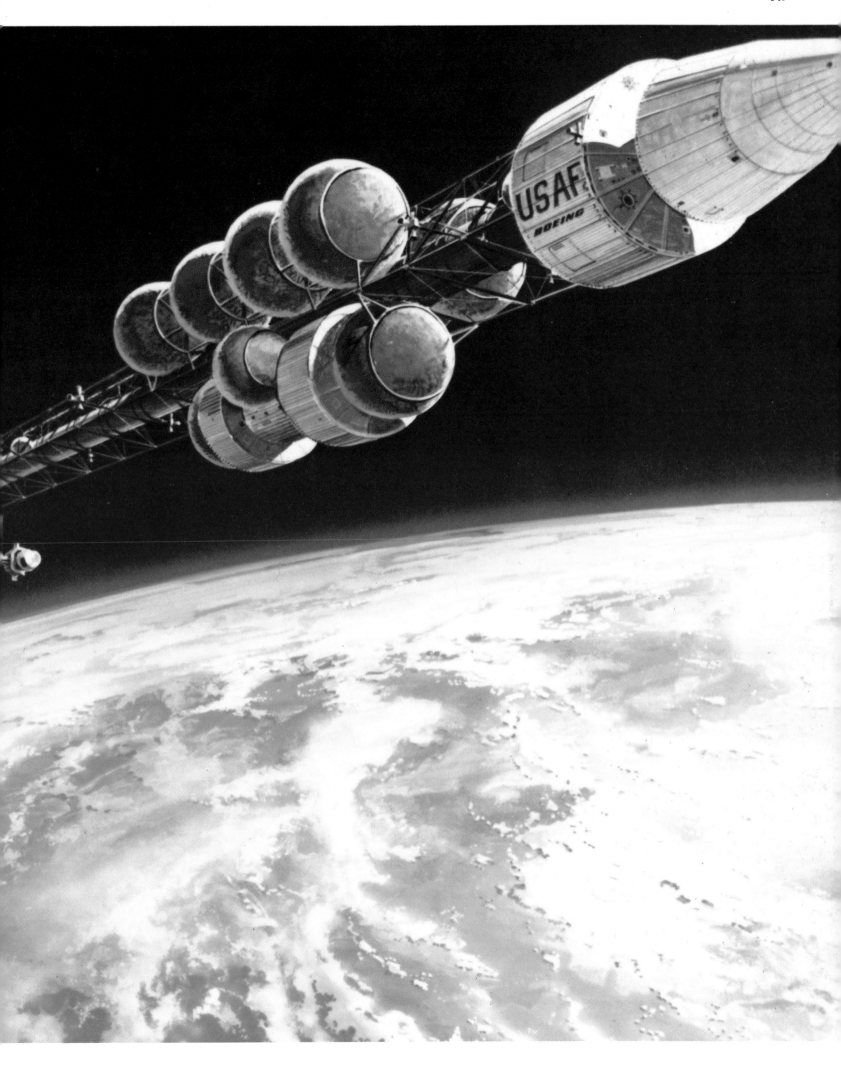

SDI SURVIVAL AND INNOVATION

The SDI Survivability, Lethality and Key Technologies (SLKT) program has been designed to be able to address those key factors. In order to accomplish this task, the SLKT program funds research in five specific areas. The first area is Systems Survivability. The goal here is to develop technologies and tactics to enhance the survivability of defense system assets in hostile environments. The second area is known as Lethality and Target Hardening. The purpose of this project is to predict the potential vulnerability of enemy targets. Many potential targets may, as a result of SDI publicity, be 'hardened' to prevent destruction by either directed-energy weapons or kinetic energy weapons. An effective system should be capable of defending against those targets as well. The third area of research is one of Space Power and Power Conditioning. Many of the defense system components currently envisioned will require large amounts of power for operation. This presents a significant technical challenge for powering those assets which are spacebased. The research in this area is intended to co-ordinate and stimulate the development of spacebased energy generation for SDI components. The fourth area deals with materials and structures. Some of the future spacebased assets of SDI are likely to be large platforms for either weapons or sensor devices. There is very little known about possible best materials for these structures or even how they can be erected. The intent of this research element is to come to grips with the problems of large-scale structures in space. The fifth SLKT research area involves space transportaion and support. If the components of the defense system are to be spacebased, a cost efficient method for space logistics is mandatory. This goes beyond simply getting equipment into orbit. It also includes repair of equipment, rearming if necessary and of course, building new equipment.

Each of these elements of SLKT will help address the practicality of deploying a defense system. With this in mind, our review of the Strategic Defense Initiative must include some understanding of the elements of the SLKT research areas.

The System Survivability Project investigates concepts and technologies designed to test and (as much as possible) verify the potential longevity of a deployed defensive system. The effort includes not only the survivability of the initial system, but also the components which could follow. Specifically, the objectives of this project are threefold: first, to determine potential defense suppression techniques which could be used to disable or severely degrade the planned capabilities of the defensive system; second, to investigate promising active and passive survivability techniques; and third, to assist the SDI System Architecture in the development of a defense system architecture which includes as many active-passive survivability technologies as practical.

In the sketch *above,* Kinetic Kill Vehicles deploy from the spacebased launch platform *at upper right* and speed toward their targets.

In its broadest interpretation, survivability for SDI purposes means that, after dedicated attacks have been made to suppress the defense, there still remains sufficient capability to destroy a ballistic missile threat. In other words, survivability is really a measure of how the defense functions (what capabilities remain) after a direct attack on the system. This is a sort of holistic approach and does not depend (or at least should not depend) on the survival of individual defense components.

From a military perspective, survivability must include not only system capabilities, but also planning and tactics to best utilize the resources available at any one time. The System Survivability project is intended to assist the SDI System Architect in the development of a defensive system which takes as much into account as possible. Every system designed represents some compromises in terms of how it will operate, and the best system overall is one in which the shortcomings in one area are offset by the strengths of another. At this point in the Strategic Defense Initiative program, the survivability project has only just begun to work, and most of the project recommendations will likely be classified. However, some elements of the project are open to public access and are important to our understanding of SDI.

The very first major accomplishment of this project was the consolidation of relevant Defense Department survivability research into SDI projects. Apparently, when the System Survivability Project was initiated, there were more than a few similar programs operating under the auspices of the Department of Defense. These included survivability research programs for ground systems, airborne systems, as well as space systems. Much of this research was related to SDI, but not specifically oriented to SDI objectives.

The systems architecture of SDI will need to consider not only near-term systems components. It must evolve to be able to incorporate future technology. The survivability research program must show a similar balance so that proper technical concepts mature with the system. Initial research in survivability technologies has already produced some promising concepts. Accordingly, a multiyear technology development and test program was designed to support the needs of the system as it evolves. So far this research has established the role which some technologies will play in the strategic defense system. Yet to be done in the near term is the design and development of experiments to test the component hardening techniques required for survival.

A significant concern for SDI planners is the effect of nuclear explosions in space. Obviously, the defense system components nearby would be destroyed no matter how protected it was. The concern is for equipment which survives the effect of the detonation. The surge of electromagnetic power across almost all frequencies is sufficient to disable most electronic components. The hardening of electronic components and major subsystems is a prime effort. To date, SDI researchers have developed several devices to protect electronics from electromagnetic surges. Also considered in this 'hardening' area are system optics: if a laser mirror relay system were ever deployed for SDI, the surfaces of all operational mirrors would necessarily be hardened from the effects of nuclear radiation.

In order to effectively 'design in' system survivability, it is important that system architects have some idea of what potential countermeasures could be used against the system. The survivability efforts have resulted in an initial compiling of detailed threat scenarios. These scenarios describe the various possible responses an adversary could make in order to counter the proposed strategic defense system.

These countermeasures and possible survivability techniques are prepared by the three team analysis group which we have met earlier. The principal elements of the countermeasure analysis program are the 'Red Team,' the 'Blue Team' and the 'Mediator Team.' The major objective of the Red Team is the formulation of a reasonable global response to a United States strategic defense system. This response is a set

of adversary priorities specifically aimed at countering—either technically or politically—the SDI program. From a technical perspective, the Red Team will examine system concepts to circumvent such defenses as boost and postboost intercepts or midcourse decoying tactics.

Each Red Team will work with a corresponding Blue Team to evaluate results. The Blue Team objective is primarily to assess the impact of the Red Team countermeasures on the design of the defense system.

The Mediator Teams in this effort are made up of senior military and government technicians who are experienced in the realities of strategic offense and defense. Their task is to review the efforts of the Red and Blue Teams and assess the credibility and implications of countermeasure threats.

The efforts of all three teams are provided to SDI architects for incorporation in the ever-evolving system plan. This method of critical analysis ensures that the United States strategic defense system will be well designed and useful.

The survivability study also has a limited budget for experimentation. If a particularly strong countermeasures option comes out of the Red/Blue/Mediator Team analysis, it may be necessary to see if that countermeasure is technically feasible.

The next area of importance in the SLKT program is that of Lethality and Target Hardening (LTH). The objective of this project is to determine the destructive force (lethality)

which can be inflicted by the weapons under consideration for the defense system. This study includes (or tries to include) as many types of targets as may be encountered by the defense. The purpose of this effort is to determine the vulnerability of offensive systems to potential defense system weaponry. The LTH project is heavily oriented to experimentation and the generation of basic scientific data. Project experimental data is expected to prove the lethality of defense system weapons against both hardened and unhardened targets. Experiments will be conducted at various facilities participating in the SDI research effort.

The High Energy Laser System Test Facility (HELSTF) at the White Sands Missile Range is being used to assess ICBM booster vulnerability to high intensity continuous wave (chemical type) lasers. A particle beam test facility has been developed at the Brookhaven National Laboratory to assess the lethality of these beams on various targets.

Thus far, the LTH efforts have accomplished a long list of lethality experiments. These include studies of the effect of X rays on laser mirrors; microwave weapons (microwaves may be able to damage electronic components of missiles and their warheads); and the impact effects of hyper-velocity

The High Energy Laser Test Facility at White Sands Missile Range (*below left and right,* and *at right*) is being used to determine missile vulnerability to high intensity continuous wave lasers, and is part of SDI's Lethality and Target Hardening (LTH) project.

plastic projectile traveling at about four miles per second (roughly 15,000 miles per hour).

The results of the LTH project will not only benefit defense systems weapon designers, but could also be a tremendous aid to any scientist concerned with system survivability. The hardening measures found to be effective in LTH experiments could well be used in the detailed design of defense system components. As a result, all LTH efforts are closely coordinated with the system survivability project. Further, such hardening techniques could also be usefully applied to the offensive endeavor of the United States. With this in mind, LTH efforts are co-ordinated with complementary efforts in other military areas.

Some of the weapons concepts currently under consideration by the Strategic Defense Initiative Organization will require a significant amount of electrical energy for operation. While this is not a major concern for groundbased systems, spaceborne applications must be capable of long-term, independent operation. The Power and Power Conditioning Project was established to develop power generation and conditioning technologies capable of providing electric power for the projected need of the defense. To keep a perspective on this issue, note that even this early in the SDI effort, power levels in excess of hundreds of megawatts have already been attained.

This challenging project is divided into two basic areas: power requirements and mission studies, and assessment and evaluation of candidate concepts. The first task of the Power and Power Conditioning effort is to compile a requirements list for all potential defense system components now under consideration. This list will necessarily be one which requires periodic updating in order to remain abreast of current system concepts. SDIO has formed an Independent Evalua-

tion Group to review various candidate power system concepts, evaluate the technical merits of each and co-ordinate the more promising concepts with other SDI projects.

One of the most interesting efforts of the Power and Power Conditioning Project is the SP-100 task. In 1983, the United States began a project, jointly managed by the Department of Energy (DOE), the Defense Advanced Research Projects Agency (DARPA) and the National Aeronautics and Space Administration (NASA) to develop a compact nuclear power system for use in space. This power system, a liquid metal cooled, fast-spectrum reactor, is envisioned as a 300 kilowatt generator which is to have a life expectancy of 10 years and will have the potential to grow to the one megawatt level. The SP-100 technology is planned to be used not only for defense system needs, but also as a baseline for several non-SDI military and NASA applications under consideration for the next decade. The SP-100 design will undergo a major subsystem (reactor, power conversion, heat transport and radiator, and controls) ground test in the near future at the Hanford Engineering Development Laboratory. The testing will involve demonstration of performance, safety, dependability, manufacturability, and technology readiness. It is expected that the final design will be completed in 1991. The system is considered essential by the US Air Force and Navy as the power source for spacebased, wide-area surveillance radar.

Also under consideration for the Power and Power Conditioning Project is a multimegawatt research task. This effort is designed to address the power required for both high-level

The four photos *below, left to right* depict the launch sequence phase of a FLAGE kill vehicle guidance system test at White Sands on 14 November 1984. *At above right* is an artist's concept of a spacebased nuclear power station for SDI orbital systems.

continuous power as well as for 'burst-mode' power. Both nuclear and nonnuclear power sources will be considered for this task. The goal is to establish and advance the technology base by the early 1990s in order to deliver a potential system which satisfies the mission requirements at a reasonable cost.

A third interesting power-related task is Pulsed Power Conditioning Technology. This effort addresses the special energy and delivery requirements of the weapons systems under consideration. Pulsed power technology is used to condition raw power to match the requirements of a given load. The effort will seek to develop elements capable of delivering sufficient energy pulses to drive the many different (as yet conceptual) weapons and sensors.

In the Fletcher Study, and early in the SDI research program, there was a recognized need for research and development in the areas of materials and large structures in space. It was clear that a variety of systems and technologies critical to the success of the envisioned defense system would not succeed if there were not improvements in this area. For example, major but lightweight platforms required for use in space would depend on employment and maintenance of large structures. Materials and structures technology does not exist to the degree required for the survivability of SDI system assets.

Early on in the SDI effort, it was believed that this particular technology would be an offshoot of the work being done in other areas of defense research. This was not the case, however, and it soon became clear that the effort needed the stimulus of a specific project. In short, this activity lags behind other efforts within SDI.

Research is now being conducted by the DOD, the DOE and NASA. The SDIO has recently initiated an assessment study to determine the type of material and structures which would be required in support of current defense system concepts. Further, because this area lags behind the others, there will also be an analysis of current projects—both within the SDI effort and elsewhere—that are relevant to the Materials and Structures Project. With this area now getting the attention of a specific project, it is likely that there will soon be rapid advances in the field.

The economic feasibility of a multilayered ballistic missile defense system may well depend on the ability to reduce the cost of establishing and maintaining (that is, deploy, supply and repair as necessary) such a system in space. The Space Transportation and Support Project funds the investigation of the space logistics and technologies required to support an extensive space force of the magnitude and complexity envisioned by the SDI planners. Areas of investigation include 'heavy-lift' launch vehicles, orbit-to-orbit transfer systems, on-orbit assembly and servicing, robotics, advanced technology propulsion, command and control systems.

Recently, a joint NASA/SDI Space Transport and Support study determined that two-stage, fully reusable manned and unmanned launch vehicles can provide flexible and cost effective access to space. However, developing these vehicles will require significant investment in both technology and new facilities. Study findings included the following key points: a new manned shuttle will be needed by the turn of the century; there is a substantial need for an orbital maneuvering vehicle with a robotic front end; and an un-

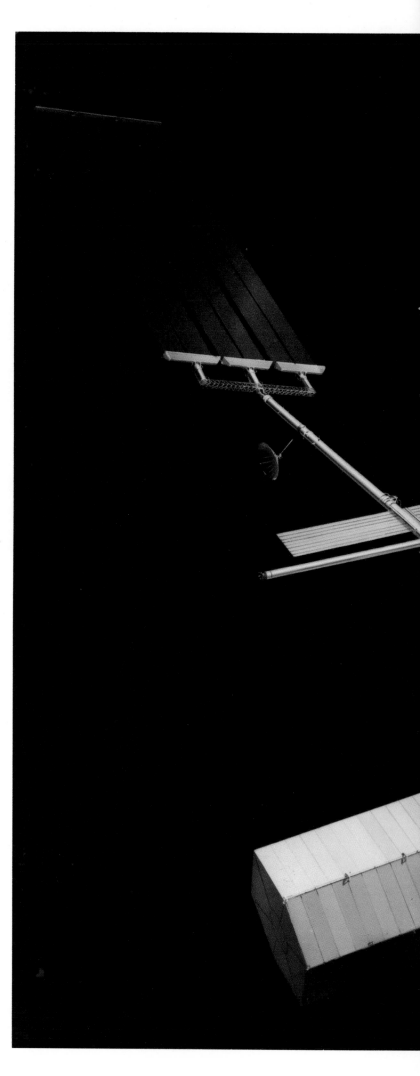

Supplying a weapons platform (*at right*) will be relatively easy with such a tool as the Shuttle Orbiter, and would be easier still if an actual space plane—which is analogous to an orbit-capable jetliner—is developed as planned by US aerospace manufacturers.

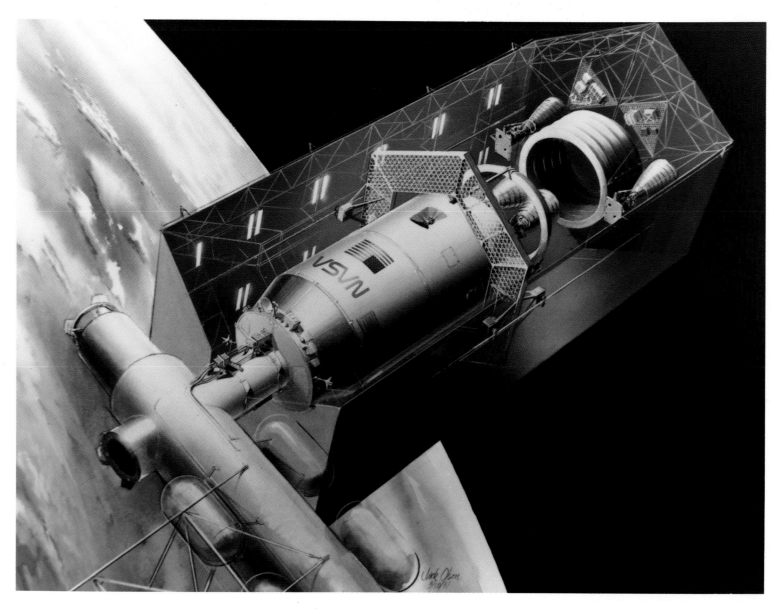

manned, partly reusable cargo vehicle capable of 30 launches per year and with three times the shuttle payload capacity could, by the mid to late 1990s deliver satellites to low Earth orbit at half the current cost. The study also found that the most cost effective replacement for the present US launch capability would be a combination of a manned vehicle and a fully reusable, unmanned cargo vehicle. These vehicles could be used, depending on deployment decisions, to lift in excess of 1,000,000 pounds per year by the late 1990s. This cargo would be placed in low earth orbit for defense system architectures dominated by the deployment of kinetic energy weapon systems.

One other Space Transportation and Support Project task is worthy of note. The SDIO is a participant in the National Aerospace Plane (NASP) research program which is now underway. This vehicle is envisioned to operate from conventional runways and to go into space; orbit; and deorbit on command after travelling in the Mach 8 to Mach 15 speed range (8 to 15 times the speed of sound). NASP is viewed as the natural successor to the shuttle transport system and has two key advantages: first, it could provide almost instant access to space; and second, it is targeted to reduce the cost of orbiting payloads to about 20 percent of the cost of using the shuttle (in other words, a targeted cost of about $200 per pound).

The most significant challenge to NASP is propulsion. It is likely that the vehicle will require three types of engine

Boeing's Trans Atmospheric Vehicle (the triangular craft in the sketch *at right*) is a conceptual spaceplane. The Future Orbital Transfer Vehicle (FOTV), an orbital cargo bus conceptualized *above* as being maintenanced in its orbital hangar, would supply SDI platforms.

systems. Each system would be suited to a different flight envelope: there would likely be an engine system for takeoff, another for supersonic flight and another for space operations (orbit insertion, maneuvering, and deorbit burns). The most aggressive goal for NASP is to be flying by the mid 1990s with a development cost on the order of several billion dollars.

The Survivability, Lethality and Key Technologies portion of SDI certainly does not gain the publicity of some of the better-known programs. However, the efforts and accomplishments in this program will have a direct bearing on the eventual success of the United States Strategic Defense System.

One final element of the Strategic Defense Initiative remains, the Innovative Science and Technology (IST) Office. This office is a technical division within the SDIO and is charged with the task of seeking new and innovative approaches to ballistic missile defense. A research and development department (within a research and development organization), IST allocates funding to sponsor research.

The IST research efforts support the SDI effort by establishing a technology base by way of fundamental research throughout the scientific community. This includes univer-

sities, government and national laboratories, small businesses and large industries. Through this research funding, the IST funding both provides a service and reaps a reward. Historically, many breakthroughs in science and engineering have come from university research programs. IST can help those programs along and at the same time, further the efforts of the SDIO by applying those breakthroughs to defense applications. IST also administers the SDIO Small Business Innovation Research (SBIR) program. This federally-mandated program requires that a minimum of one percent of the total IST funding for research and development be allocated to small businesses. Hopefully, this funding will also generate breakthroughs.

Overall, the science and engineering funding from IST falls into five major categories. The first is advanced, high-speed computing. We have already noted the need for powerful computers and software. The BM/C^3 function of SDI will determine the effectiveness of the entire defense system. As a result of the IST funding, a program exists in optical data processing. Recently, a major breakthrough occurred in the effort to construct an optical supercomputer. An overseas institution is willing to join with IST and American researchers to further develop this optically switched computer.

The second major IST funding category deals with materials and structures. We noted earlier that primary research in this area has lagged behind other SDI efforts. Recently, a new composite material—a lithium alumina silicate glass, reinforced with silicon carbide fibers—was fabricated. This new material is lightweight, laser resistant and has very high tensile strength. The properties of this material make it very promising for space structure application.

IST also funds research in sensing and discrimination. Although the SDI program related to Surveillance, Acquisition, Tracking and Kill Assessment (SATKA) is making great strides in this area, some IST efforts have proven very fruitful. A new microminiature refrigerator the size of a quarter has been developed that can cool a niobium nitride superconductor to 10 degrees Kelvin (almost -450 degrees F!). Used in a germanium infrared detector, this remarkable little device has its refrigerator fluid conducted by a novel mechanical pump which can be powered by the heat escaping from a space system. This miniature cryogenic cooler could possibly be used in the fabrication of a novel, low cost, broad band infrared detector needed to perform some of the many sensing tasks required for the defense system.

Another area of IST funding is in the area of advanced space power. Two IST-funded advances are worthy of attention. A new insulating polymer made from resins of vinylidene fluoride and tetrafluoreothylene, has been designed for use in new, high energy-density, supercapacitors. This polymer was designed entirely by computer simulation and then synthesized in a laboratory. Other new supercapacitors for power storage have been developed. These supercapacitors can store up to 50 kilojoules of energy in a can the size of a wastebasket (the joule equals one watt-second—the energy released in one second by a current of one ampere through a resistance of one ohm). This sort of energy device could have many applications in the DEW and KEW programs. This supercapacitor is aimed at pushing the frontier of capacitor design. An immediate goal is the production of 250 kilojoules of energy in the same wastebasket-size cannister as the current 50 KJ capacitor. A three year goal for that wastebasket is a megajoule.

Many ideas for space stations abound—the one *at left* shows a 'dual keel' Power Tower Station, which would serve as a power and communications center for various SDI technologies. These mute antennae (*above*) are part of the DOD's satellite tracking and control network.

The IST Nuclear Power Consortium has a plan to design a multimegawatt pulsed gaseous fuel reactor. The advantage of this type of reactor is that the gas can be pulsed rapidly through a system. It is hoped that this type of reactor will attain the 'burst mode' power requirements needed for DEW and KEW programs.

The final area of IST funding is in directed and kinetic energy concepts. Two particularly interesting efforts have resulted from the funding. The first is a major program at the Lawrence Livermore National Laboratory to develop an X-ray laser. This X-ray laser effort has definite applications to DEW planning, plus it has the advantage of being more than a 'one shot' weapon (as is the X-ray laser which is driven by a nuclear explosion). The second effort was a major breakthrough on the way to developing a gamma ray laser. Working in the area of Mossbauer spectroscopy, a researcher discovered it was possible to compensate for the nucleus recoil caused by gamma ray emission (the 'Mossbauer effect' deals with the phenomenon resulting from the interaction of atomic nuclei and gamma rays) by employing an external laser as an additional photon source. Although a gamma ray laser is still a long way off, the potential for this research is excellent. At the current time, the only way to create a gamma ray laser is through the use of a nuclear explosive device to pump the laser.

The funding supplied by IST is in primary research areas, but there is certainly the promise that basic research breakthroughs will lead to rapid advances in the overall scheme of strategic defense. There is no doubt that other areas of the SDI program will contribute to more than their share of the headlines. However, the real future of the defense system lies with the quiet efforts of the scientists in the Innovative Science and Technology program.

PUTTING THE DEFENSE TOGETHER

The Strategic Defense Initiative is at this point simply a lot of research and development projects, costing a lot of money. The various and sundry pieces of the entire program add up to little more than a vision of the future. In 1983, President Reagan asked the scientific community to 'turn their great talents now to the cause of mankind and world peace, to give us the means of rendering nuclear weapons obsolete.'

We have seen the pieces which would one day make up the 'means' of which the president spoke. We have also seen the challenges which must be overcome to make the components work. But what of the system itself? How will the pieces be assembled to achieve the goal? The system architects of the SDIO have the challenging, perhaps even unenviable, task of fitting all of the pieces of the research and development puzzle into a cohesive, flexible and realistic design.

Fitting the pieces together may not be as difficult as will be the logistical and political questions and constraints which must be addressed along the way. Even so, the design team must take into consideration that some components will be operationally ready years before others. The planners must structure the system to allow for evolution of equipment based on research completion estimates. In other words, the system must have the capability of being expanded from a rudimentary to a full-fledged strategic defense system when-

ever technology and funding allows. Through it all, these system designers will be constrained by a variety of treaties and agreements. The United States does not want other countries to break away from their obligations with us. Nor should we walk away from ours with them.

We have seen the components with which the system architects must work. Given a decision to deploy, how might the system evolve? The answer to this question will likely not be known for some years to come (indeed, the SDIO is looking to the early part of the next decade for the first opportunity for a deployment decision). If a decision to deploy were made, however, how would the architects go about the task of assembling the pieces into a workable whole? Although the SDIO isn't talking about this aspect of the project, they have provided enough information for us to try to assemble the system ourselves.

In November of 1985, the SDIO presented an unclassified version of the presently favored design. In this concept, the system consisted of seven roughly independent layers of defensive interceptors. Each layer would be designed to permit no more than about 20 percent of the offensive targets to pass through. In this architecture, there would be two layers of weapons to attack missiles in the boost and postboost stages. One of these layers would be directed-energy weapons, while the other would consist of kinetic energy

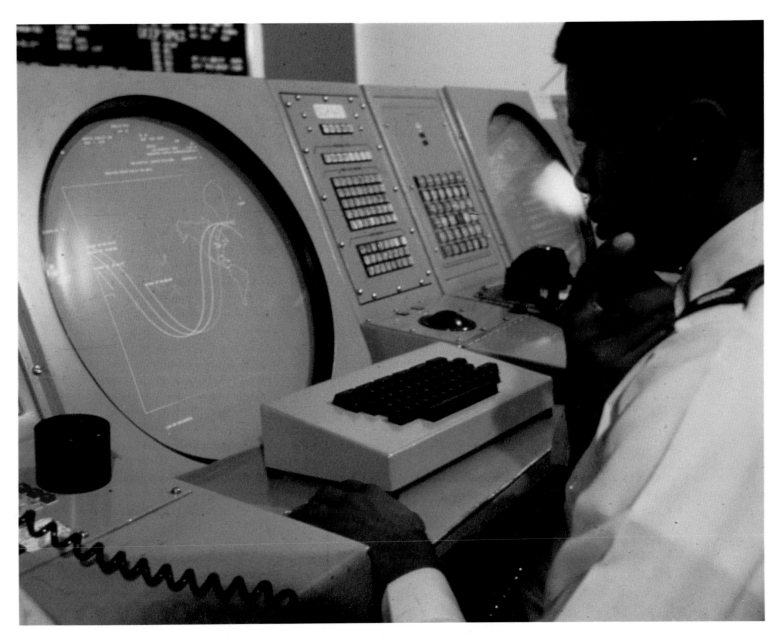

Seemingly mundane, the ground traces on this NORAD radar screen (*above*) are what it's all about—to identify an object, determine its position and attempt to interpret what it's doing up there; and to make your own orbital systems do what they're supposed to do.

devices. There would be three layers of weapons to defend in the midcourse phase of an ICBM trajectory. Directed- and kinetic energy weapons would occupy two of the layers. The third layer is undetermined at this point. However, this third layer could be a groundbased laser system or, according to SDIO, devices which would discharge masses of pellets or aerosols in the hope of destroying decoys. Finally, there would be two layers of groundbased rocket interceptors to contend with any reentry vehicles which penetrate the previous defensive layers.

Now then, with this picture of a potential system assembly, how will the architects go about the task of deployment? For us to be able to deploy a hypothetical system, we will need to make two basic assumptions. First, at some point in the future existing treaty and agreement constraints will be modified, such that there will be no restrictions on the deployment of this system. Second, the system will be deployed in its entirety, and there will be no consideration given to delays or setbacks in development. Given these assumptions, the following is an attempt at a deployment scenario:

In the early years of the next decade, the initial components of the defensive system will come on line. These first components will consist of three elements. First, we shall see the completion of construction of several terminal imaging radar systems (TIR). These first radar systems will augment

the existing early warning devices and will conform with the limitations of the 1972 Treaty (they will be located along the periphery of the national territory and must be oriented outward). At the same time, we will see the operational start of the Airborne Optical System (AOS). The early deployments will be aboard the same platform on which the system was tested (a Boeing 767). This platform will be deployed plurally, in squadrons near areas which are suspected to be strategic areas for an aggressor. These AOS squadrons would work in concert with the first layer of the TIR site.

Finally, in this first strategic defense system deployment, we would see the addition of chemically-fueled endo- and exoatmospheric interceptor missiles. These would be kinetic energy weapons much like the equipment used in the Homing Overlay Experiment. These interceptors would be clustered at key points around the nation (and eventually around the world to help protect our allies) and would be equipped with infrared and radar detection homing devices.

Clearly, the first deployment of our defense system would be completely groundbased. The reason for groundbased deployments are twofold. First, our earliest defense system

technology would be best monitored from ground sites. The capability to put equipment in Earth orbit for extended periods will take more time and research to perfect. Second, the obligations of existing treaties, specifically the 1972 ABM Treaty, would continue to be met through ground-basing of defense components. This first deployment would in effect be the terminal defense system—of the eventual extended strategic defense system.

Although this first deployment would add to defensive capabilities, there would be little need to improve the command and control system. The interceptor systems would require only the addition of a Battle Management system to bring the software up to speed. The difficulty, however, is the requirement to have a Battle Management/Command, Control and Communication (BM/C³) system which can evolve along with the strategic defense network. This means that the BM/C³ must be prepared as a framework for the future. In other words, the BM/C³ architecture must be designed to accept each new addition to the defense system with ease. The technically easiest time for the addition of the defense hardware (the KEW interceptors) is also the time for what is perhaps one of the most technically difficult software efforts. The future success of the defensive system demands that the BM/C³ architecture be almost entirely future oriented.

Before the end of this century, the defense alert system will be expanded. A series of sensor platforms will be launched and placed in an orbit which will allow full-time coverage of the ICBM launch sites as well as much of the ocean area of the world. Coverage of the oceans is intended to do more than monitor surface fleets. Defense system planners also want to be able to 'spot' submarines. At present, submarines must approach the surface in order to receive communications signals. Submarines are most vulnerable when they are close to the surface. Spaceborne sensors also 'look' at the water pattern to find submarines. A sub traveling at a depth churns up cold water which, when combined with warmer water above, creates a coldwater wake. The wake can be easily detected by the infrared sensing equipment aboard a satellite. Beyond the difference in wake temperature, satellites can also spot submarines by watching for disturbances in the sea state. The irregular wave pattern of the sea can be broken by the underwater wake of a submerged vehicle. Special satellite radar can measure and track the sea state with a fine degree of precision.

The network of orbiting sensing devices would be placed in an orbital path which is neither geosynchronous nor random: both of these orbits have predictable tracks and allow the possibility of an aggressor predicting 'holes' in the surveillance coverage. Instead, the orbits would have to be relative to other satellites in the system and therefore hopefully prevent 'holes' in the coverage. It is at this point that a provision of the ABM Treaty will definitely need to be modified. The current treaty specifically states that 'each Party undertakes not to . . . deploy ABM systems or components which are . . . spacebased.' It is possible that the treaty would have been modified for the deployment of the Airborne Optical System, but that depends somewhat on the reading and interpretation of the treaty.

As discussed in an earlier section, these sensors will be capable of detecting the launch 'signatures' of ICBMs as

Orbital sensors help facilities like this PAVE PAW Space Command Center (*left*) to keep tabs on Soviet nuclear submarine activities.

they lift off (in other words, still in the boost phase of flight). Since the only interceptors available at this point are the KEW interceptors deployed in phase one of the rollout, the earliest that we could hope to eliminate the offensive threat is in the late midcourse portion of the ICBM trajectories. This being the case, a launch detected at this time in the deployment of the defense system would still trigger the Mutually Assured Destruction (MAD) sequence with which we have lived so long. Depending upon the launch sites and trajectories of the offensive missiles, the sensors will have as much as 30 minutes to discriminate targets from decoys and compute trajectories.

The Battle Management system will take on a bigger role in the defensive system at this point. Using the sensors to track the threat, the BM/C³ system will be required to assign interceptors and determine optimum launch windows for the best possible 'kill' opportunity.

Clearly, through the second phase of the deployment, there is still a fear of MAD. There is still the real possibility that the defensive system could be overwhelmed by a massive attack. Ten to 15 years from now we will still be living under the threat of nuclear destruction.

Soon after the establishment of the orbiting sensor network (right around the turn of the 21st century), phase three will begin. In phase three we will see the groundbased free-electron laser systems come on line. This effort will be a large undertaking because of the need to position mirrors and small low power lasers in space. The optics would consist of several larger mirrors which would be used to relay the laser beam plus smaller mission or fighting mirrors which would recline the beam from the relay mirror, focus it and direct it to the target. The low power lasers would be used to test atmospheric conditions prior to propagating the weapon-strength laser beam.

With this addition of hardware, the BM/C³ system will take on a new importance. The requirement of target selection, assignment of targeting priorities and interception will become very important to the success of the system. This becomes somewhat complicated because of the need to pass on trajectory and fire control data to the various laser sites. Further, once the laser is 'fired' at a target, the BM/C³ system must determine if there is a need to shoot again at the target. This requires continued sensor tracking, communication and analysis. The BM/C³ system must also alert the groundbased KEW interceptors just in case some ballistic missiles or reentry vehicles make it past the range of the laser systems.

With the addition of the groundbased laser systems, the defense network has a true midcourse intercept capability. The key to the addition of the lasers is advancements in beam power-density and optics technology. The defensive system is now capable of a variety of responses to offensive threats. More importantly, the addition of the groundbased laser systems relieves the pressure on the terminal defense network (the KEW chemically fueled interceptor missiles) and could mean its success.

Thus far in the building of the strategic defense system, the shuttle transportation system and unmanned cargo launch vehicles have provided the lifting power to get the components into space. By the year 2010, the National Aerospace Plane (NASP) will be brought into service. This craft—with its capability to takeoff from a runway, go into space and return—will open the door to a rapid expansion of space activities.

Above: The control center of the Defense Meteorological Satellite Programs, near Fairchild AFB. Shown *at right* is the launching of the sixth flight of a FLAGE weapon—*see the photos on page 144* for more on this successful first target test in the FLAGE program.

The first priority for NASP will be to take part in the upgrading of the defense system sensors. Using advanced materials ferried by the NASP, the sensors will be expanded to become complex sensor platforms complete with an array of detection devices to monitor the full electromagnetic spectrum. These sensor platforms will give the defense all the capability needed to monitor an offensive threat from birth (launch) to death (intercept).

At this time the BM/C³ system will require modification. The additional discrimination capabilities of the enhanced sensor platforms will provide the Battle Management system with a wealth of raw data which must be analyzed, acknowledged and processed. This improvement in information will greatly enhance the quality of data provided by the system and enable military commanders to make informed decisions about defensive threats.

Close behind the sensor platform upgrade, the weapons system will receive an addition. This new component will be spacebased, chemically fueled KEW interceptor missiles. These interceptors will support the system's midcourse coverage which was previously handled almost exclusively by the groundbased free-electron laser system. These KEW networks will be placed in a variety of orbital paths. The mix of orbits will give the spacebased weapons an elusive look.

The weapons in the defense system now include the mature technology groundbased KEW interceptors, the groundbased free-electron laser system, and the 'next generation'

spacebased KEW interceptors. These weapons, combined with the groundbased radar and the newly upgraded space-based sensor platforms provide, for the first time, the feel of an integrated multilayered defense. In reality, the system now has at least four layers of defense against ballistic missiles.

Spacebased lasers will be deployed around 2015. Using the NASP to ferry parts into orbit, these laser systems will be built onto newly fabricated weapons platforms. These platforms will have propulsion devices for maneuverability. Further, the platforms will be designed in such a way that they may be linked with other platforms (for additional power density through the combined use of more than one laser beam). The various laser weapons platforms will be based in a series of orbits depending upon mission. Some will be positioned to defend against midcourse-phase reentry vehicles in support of the KEW interceptors and the groundbased lasers. Others will be oriented near ICBM launch sites and will provide the first real launch and postboost phase interception capability. Further, these boostphase intercept systems will mark the operational start of a full coverage, multi-layered ballistic missile defense system.

This stage will be the most complex for the BM/C³ system. With the addition of laser weapons platforms, the defensive network has a new dimension available. The orbiting assets of the system may now be assembled into logical battle groups depending on their proximity to an engagement location. The BM/C³ system must now be able to 'juggle' the assets of the defense into battle groups, track targets, assign targets to individual weapons stations and assess the status of each threat and system asset. The BM/C³ system capabilities will determine the strength of the overall strategic defense.

Around 2020, two new weapons systems will be added to the defensive system. The first will be the hypervelocity rail gun, and the other will be the neutral particle beam. These weapons systems will be assembled in space and either combined with the already existing laser weapons platforms or on independent fight platforms. The variety of weapons stations increases the flexibility of the defense system, and the rail gun can be used for defense against ballistic missiles or as

Seen *at left* is the Los Alamos National Laboratories' concept of a space station featuring a massive solar panel array, ensuring it lots of power. *Below* is another conceptual source of SDI orbital power—the 100 kilo-watt SP-100 nuclear space reactor.

defense against attempts at suppression. The neutral particle beam can also play a dual role. The particle beam can be used as a weapon to disrupt the electronics of offensive missiles and as was discussed earlier, the beam can also be used as a sensor to discriminate reentry vehicles from decoys in the midcourse phase of a ballistic missile trajectory.

A few more years will pass before the final components are added to the defense system. These components, probably the most powerful elements of the system, will be X-ray and gamma ray laser devices added to the asset base between 2025 and 2030. Unlike the current vision of this type of weapon, these will not be driven by the explosion of a nuclear device. Rather, they would be beams propagated by laser-like devices and have a 'multishot' capability much like the space-based laser system installed a few years earlier. These X-ray and gamma ray beam devices will either disrupt the electronic components of reentry vehicles and ballistic missiles, or destroy them entirely by the 'shock' of the beam striking the surface of the target.

These final (for the purposes of our scenario, at least) additions to the defense will require only simple modification to the BM/C³ software. As you will recall, the most complex change to the system came when the BM/C³ first had to recognize the dynamics of logical battle groups. This having been accomplished with a previous change, the BM/C³ system now only needs to be 'informed' of the new weapons systems at its disposal. The information required by the Battle Management system includes such things as orbital location weapons capability, intended mission (in other words, emphasis on a particular phase of a ballistic missile trajectory) and so on. In a sense, the additions to the system have almost become 'plug-in' components.

As first envisioned, the defense system is now the means to 'render nuclear weapons impotent and obsolete.' By the year 2030, nearly half a century will have passed since the announcement of a vision of a strategic defense system. Years of research, planning, challenges and technological advancement will have been required to bring the vision to fruition. The effort involved in turning the dream into a reality will have been formidable to say the very least. By 2030, the United States and its allies will have achieved a wonderful technological success. But the most important question will be whether the concept of peace which underlies the strategic system will be as successful.

SHOULD WE BUILD IT?

Success is measured in terms of goals. There is no doubt that, given the drive and inventiveness of American and allied nations' scientists, the defense system we have just imagined is attainable. Indeed it is likely that some of the fiction deployment dates are too conservative. One can only be amazed at the inventive ability of scientists and engineers.

There should be no question then of whether such a strategic defense system could be built. There is no doubt but that it could. The questions about the Strategic Defense Initiative, however, should come from other areas. These include:

1. What would happen to the strategic balance between Russia and the United States?
2. What about our allies—how would the SDI affect them?
3. How much would such a system cost?
4. Are there better alternatives?
5. Can we really rid the world of nuclear weapons?

These are the five questions which must be addressed by each of us. These are the questions which should be the deciding factors in determining whether or not we should deploy the defense system as envisioned. These are the questions which could well determine the future peace of our world. To be truly aware of the implications of the Strategic

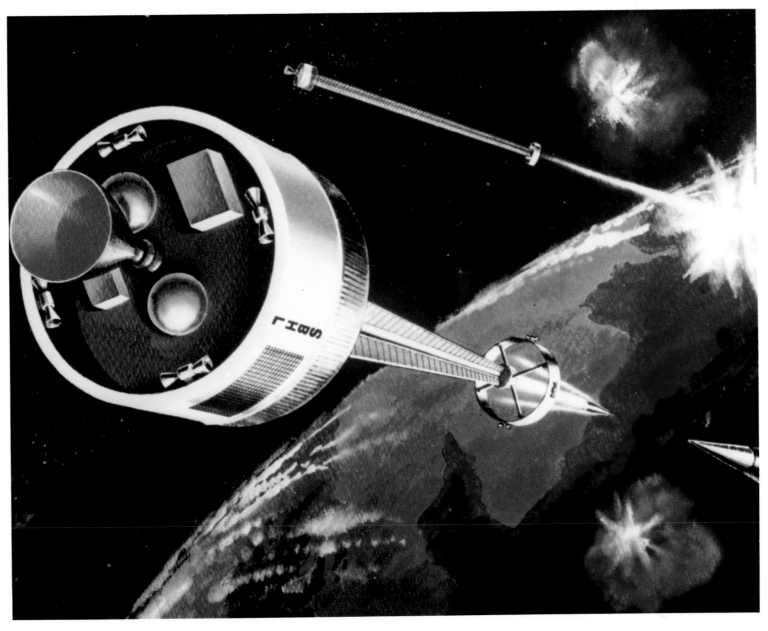

In theory, at least, we've come a long way: *At left,* a USAF SM-68 Atlas II lifts off to deliver its warhead to a target 5000 miles downrange, in 1962. The proposed spacebased railgun *above* would accelerate its projectiles to more than 20 miles per second.

Defense Initiative, we must each form a considered opinion about the nontechnical issues. The answers to these nontechnical issues should be the determining factors in a discussion to deploy (or not deploy) the SDI technologies.

The Strategic Defense Initiative is many things to many people. Some expect that a defensive system such as this will save lives. Others see it as a bargaining chip in arms control negotiations. The leaders of the Soviet Union view the SDI as a part of a United States buildup to a first-strike strategy; the Soviets see the SDI as just another element in a carefully planned American aggression strategy. They see SDI together with the B-1 bomber, Pershing missile, MX missile and the space shuttle as constituent to an ever-threatening offensive capability. No matter what our stated intentions, it is obvious to the Russians that the SDI is the final element of a first-strike capability.

Of course, we can say that their concerns are groundless. But what we must do first is consider their concern. We have already discussed the decades of mistrust and dislike which our two countries have fostered toward one another. Clearly, after a long period of time, people begin to believe their

suspicions. We are no better off. The Russians can tell us that our fears about their defense system upgrade efforts are without merit as well. Do we believe them? Certainly not! No matter what the issue here, the odds are that neither side will believe the other's expressed intention, for each can find proof of the other's 'hidden agenda.'

From a strategic point of view, space is an important theater of operations for both the Soviets and Americans. Probably one of man's earliest wartime discoveries was the advantage that higher ground offered. It is always easier to fight if the enemy must struggle upward. The situation today is no different, except that the high ground is in outer space. To attack, an aggressor wishing to use missile technology must struggle upward against a defender already in place on the high ground. Neither American nor Soviet military planners want the other to have the advantage of that high ground.

There is a potential dark side to SDI which must be recognized: it is definitely possible that it could be used offensively. No matter what our stated intentions, we must accept the fact that any opponent would not miss this fact. Anything which is based on the high ground could be used to shoot down at permanent landbased objectives. Depending on the point of view, an SDI system as conceived could be used for good or for evil.

172

Finally, even if the system were only used for defense, an opponent would still have cause to worry. A system such as SDI could be used in conjunction with an offensive nuclear missile attack. Such a system would allow our missiles to be launched against their targets, while at the same time, eliminating any possibility of an effective retaliatory strike.

But what of our so-called strategic balance? Will the SDI be a destabilizing force? The answer must be 'yes, it will.' A defensive system which provides a shield against incoming missiles must necessarily have a destabilizing effect. To put this in a different perspective, it would be the same as bringing a gun to a knife fight. There is certainly the possibility that the owner of the gun will be injured by knives, but there is a better than even chance that the owner of the gun will definitely control the fight.

For strategic defenses to be truly effective as stabilizers, they must discourage all opponents from being tempted to shoot first. If there were a less than equal balance, then the MAD spiral would return as an offense/defense/counter-measure spiral. Just as now, we would be faced with the fear that some aggressor could not keep up with the pace of the spiral and choose to shoot first.

No matter how we view it, the SDI will necessarily alter the current strategic defense balance. But what choices have we? According to US Intelligence reports, in the past 20 years the Soviet Union has spent roughly as much on defense as it has on offensive capabilities. And, as we discussed earlier, the Soviet program of advanced technology research (including

various laser and neutral particle beams) has been much larger than the US effort in terms of resources invested in physical plant and labor. This fact notwithstanding, the Soviets still have a number of reasons to fear our SDI program. The most significant cause for concern is our relative head start. Even though we lag behind the Russians in specific weapons research, a defense as envisioned requires extremely sophisticated computer systems and software—and the United States possesses the technology needed for such computer sophistication. The United States can catch up in the area of weapons research far more quickly than the Soviets can improve their computer capabilities.

So where are we? The United States has offered to discuss the implication of defensive technologies with the Soviet Union. Such a discussion would be very useful in understanding the relationship between offense, defense and the strategic balance. These discussions would also focus on how the two superpowers could put space defense systems into place. This dialogue is clearly of critical importance. Given the mistrust and suspicion with which we view one another, unless both sides deploy comparable defenses simultaneously, the side with little or no space defense capability may well decide to shoot down the space defense assets of the other side before they are fully deployed. The disastrous consequences of this scenario are what we all fear most—escalation to nuclear war.

The pride of the United States is our heritage of technological invention and superiority. This pride is well-founded and

this ability must be feared by the leaders of the Soviet Union. Indeed, the Soviets have an almost mystical fear of our technical excellence. Our ability to find a technical solution to nearly every problem is certainly proof that SDI will fly at some point in the future. Their fear of our technical ability and capability may well become the key to serious negotiations about arms reduction. Perhaps we can trade portions of the defensive system in return for stronger arms control agreements. This is, perhaps, the only viable reason for investing in the SDI effort. During the past two decades, arms control has been our only ongoing agenda with the Soviets. If SDI can be used as a negotiating chip in the high stakes game of nuclear arms, then the investment is definitely worth the trade. On the darker side, we may well be opening the door for a still greater arms race. The last attempt to deploy effective missile defenses, in the early 1970s, led to the deployment of the most feared offensive missiles in the arsenals of the world. These missiles were equipped with MIRVs (Multiple Independently targetable Reentry Vehicles) designed to overwhelm defenses by releasing a large number of warheads from a single missile. Clearly, the Russian fear of US expertise in science and technology could very well open a Pandora's box to all types of offensive and defensive weapons.

Below left: A Titan missile emerges from its silo—via elevator! *This* silo is just for storage. *Above right:* A ground crew attaches a pod of Boeing ALCM cruise missiles to the underwing of a USAF B-52. The now-defunct Minuteman Mobile Launcher concept (*below*) would have made use of extensive US rail mileage for its missile site elusiveness.

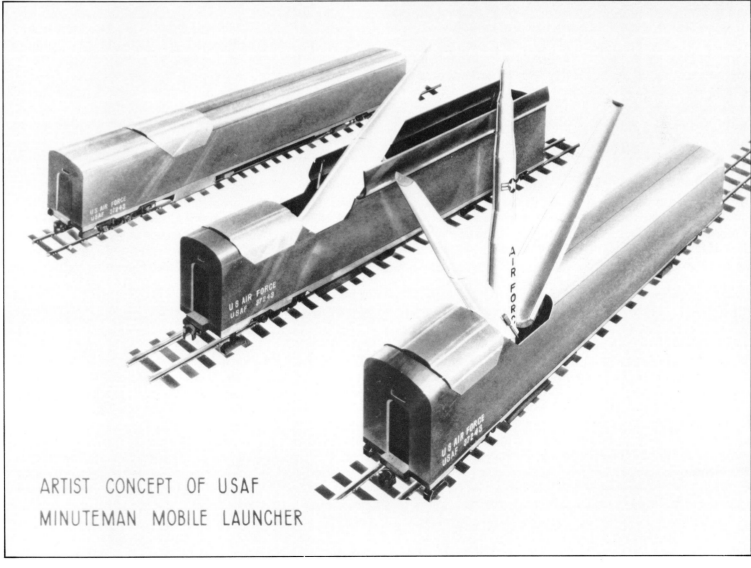

ARTIST CONCEPT OF USAF
MINUTEMAN MOBILE LAUNCHER

From the perspective of our allies, there are three major difficulties with SDI. At the top of the list is the type of defense which SDI offers. From an allied view Europe, and not the United States, is the primary focus of the political and military thinking of the Soviet Union. Indeed, in this view the United States is seen as a rear area (simply looking at a map of the world gives credibility to this perspective). This does not make the United States any less important. It does alter one's thinking about the territorial objectives however, and it also leads to different ideas about defense requirements.

If the United States and Russia develop and deploy full-scale defense systems, then (again from an allied view) Europe is vulnerable. The concern is that, whether or not the Soviet defense network is good enough to block an American attack, it will definitely be good enough to neutralize any Western European deterrent. With this in mind, Europe could well become the only nuclear battle field. This concern is even more alarming when one considers the relative weakness of the conventional NATO forces which face eastward. By most counts, the Russian forces could overwhelm those NATO forces simply by sheer numbers. The only recourse a NATO commander may have would be to escalate the conflict to the use of 'tactical' nuclear weapons.

Tactical nuclear weapons come in a variety of packages. The diversity of the threat—which includes ballistic missiles, cruise missiles, aircraft and artillery—makes European defense a more complex problem than that of defending the United States. There could be some sort of layered defense for Europe. This could include spacebased sensors, airborne Optical Adjunct Systems, exo- and endoatmospheric interceptors, interceptor aircraft, and groundbased lasers. No matter what the defensive structure, the major design objective would be to contain the level of conflict to the use of conventional forces. In other words, prevent the frightening scenario of runaway escalation to nuclear arms.

No matter how effective the US defense network, our allies probably fear the prospect of its deployment, because they would seem likely to face the burden of a 'limited tacti-

The *above* sketch depicts the first few seconds of a Soviet ICBM's eruption from its silo. *At right:* An artist's view of a Soviet dream—a convenient, reusable spacecraft. *Below right:* This conceptual Soviet space station already has its foundation in the building-block design of their manned Mir orbital module.

cal' nuclear war. The deepest fear of our allies must be that a defense of the kind discussed will likely reduce or eliminate altogether the co-operative security partnership between the United States and our Western European allies.

Canada has some specific battle-related concerns as well. Because of its proximity to Russian territory, it is definitely possible that the United States will want to postion some of the components of the defense system in Canadian territory. This would offer some early warning protection to Canada, but it would also definitely increase the likelihood that Canada may be attacked in a first strike.

The second major problem the SDI causes our allies is one of partnership. Allied participation in SDI is crucial to the design and deployment of a successful system. The United States, in light of this, intends to offer multiple contracts to European companies to study theater defense architectures. The US funding is intended to bring about a strategic defense system for Western Europe. In return for funding research, the United States would own the rights to the technology developed under SDI contract—which brings up two related problems. First, the United States is constrained by the 1972 ABM Treaty. We may not transfer SDI research, hardware or even information to other countries. So what is done for the US by a country may only be used by the US and the contracting country in the strictest reading of the treaty. For example, some countries are considered ahead of the US in certain technologies, including hypervelocity rail guns. The United States has made it quite clear that there will be no general sharing of technologies, and any sharing whatsoever would be based on a case-by-case analysis. The second problem is one of competition. Even though companies are working for the defense of their country, they are nevertheless still business competitive. It is not likely that the United States will provide companies of other countries with information

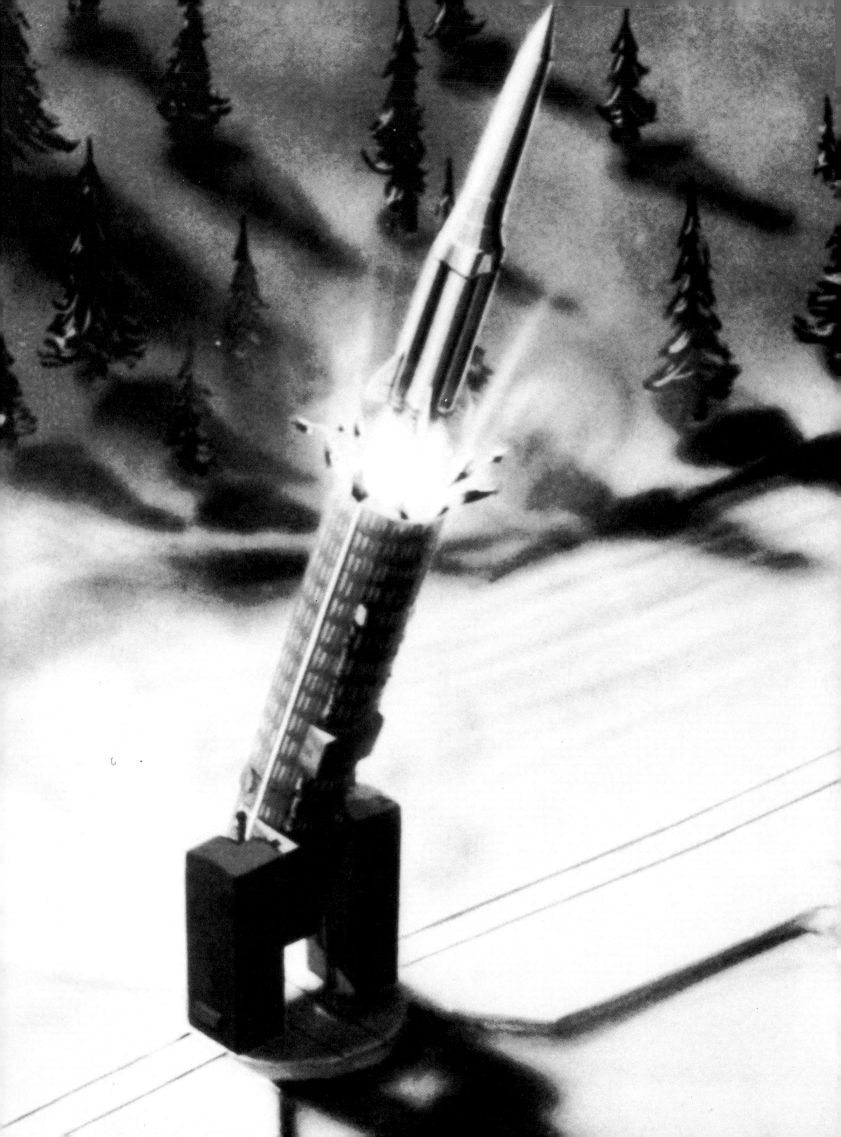

which could give them an edge in the marketplace. Our allies, as a result, see themselves giving up their best technologies (selling them, in effect) and receiving only lower-end technology sharing from the United States.

To ensure the strategic balance, we must talk with the Russians. We must recognize that negotiations will be the only means for finding a level of co-operation between the superpowers. This co-operation is an absolute necessity if we are to deploy fullscale ground- and spacebased defensive systems. In the final analysis, the desired result of the Strategic Defense Initiative will depend more on the political ingenuity of the leaders of our two nations than it will on the technical excellence of our scientists.

Although there are many other arguments to be made relative to the Soviet Union and our Strategic Defense Initiative, one point seems sparkling clear: the strategic balance between our two nations will be forever changed by the development of the SDI. Unfortunately, at this point in time we simply cannot say if this change will be for the good or the detriment of peace and stability.

Clearly, the Russians view the defense system with a dire perspective, but what about our allies? Surely they, some of whom are at the very doorstep of the Soviet Union, appreciate the opportunity which the SDI offers. The answer to this question is that SDI makes our allies almost uncomfortable as it does the Russians.

Below: An AS-4 air-to-ground missile under the wing of a Soviet Backfire bomber. *Above left:* A Soviet missile leaves its mobile launch pad in this conceptual drawing. *Above right* is the recovery stage of the test flight of an experimental Soviet spaceplane, photographed in 1983.

The third major difficulty that the Strategic Defense Initiative poses for our allies is one of 'brain drain.' It is here that our allies are between the proverbial 'rock and hard place.' If they do go along with the information-sharing SDI program, they will lose the competitive advantage of developmental rights (which would be owned by the United States). On the other hand, the amount of research underway in the United States is such that if the Allies did not participate, many of their top scientists would travel to the United States to work. It has been estimated that 46 percent of all postgraduate work in the United States is done by non-Americans. If that figure is correct, and Europe does not participate in SDI, then the number will be much larger.

Given these problems, our allies are likely to go along eventually (albeit grudgingly) with the US Strategic Defense Initiative. No doubt their participation will speed the research along. Perhaps because of their less than complete agreement, they will serve to bridge the gap between the American and Soviet camps.

No matter what support or criticism of SDI, one of the eventual topics of discussion will certainly be cost. How much will a multilayered, multifaceted strategic defense system cost? Without being facetious, the government's answer today can be summed up in one word—'depends.' The cost of the system will be a factor of time and complexity. The quicker the push for completion, the more will be the

NASA's Scout Vehicle carrying its Instrumented Test Vehicle target satellite is shown *above,* previous to its erection to launch position; *at right,* the Scout/ITV takes off: on 12 December 1985, ITV was maintained in orbit pending the actual ASAT test. *Below:* The subterranean Cheyenne Mountain Complex tracking facility.

Above: At Berkeley's Livermore Labs accelerator facility, technicians continuously make fine adjustments in system components. Los Alamos National Labs SDI experiments include the compact toroid laser project (*lower left*) and a field reverse laser energy project (*above right*).

cost to recover from mistakes and extra labor. The more layers of weapons and sensors of various kinds, the more will be the cost. Since the current research phase will cost on the order of $14 billion, some critics have guessed that the final deployment will be on the order of trillions of dollars. No matter what the guess today, it is simply too soon to tell.

There is a real fear, however, that because of the type and cost of the research, Congress will be forced into deploying all or much of the SDI technologies. This is, no doubt, a well-founded fear. It is difficult to imagine that some advanced technology would not be used after it had been invented. The history of our society would not support that sort of scenario. Rather, with the abundance of lobbyists, military contractors (both large and small) and government leaders who wholeheartedly support the SDI concept, it is more likely that some or all of SDI will be deployed. The president spoke of the leaders of some future administration deciding whether or not to deploy the SDI technologies—more likely, this will be a case of when and where and how to deploy.

To be honest, we must ask ourselves whether or not there are alternatives to SDI. There are at least three. The first is the continued dependence on Mutually Assured Destruction (MAD) diplomacy. Clearly, this is an unacceptable alternative. We have lived with it in a sort of tense, unwilling peace for so long now that we are mentally numbed by it. In the 1950s and 1960s there were air raid drills in schools, which provided a very real reminder of the possibility of war. There

are still emergency broadcast tests. We have become immune to such an extent that the average citizen does not even consider that a missile could be launched from the other side of the world and reach its target faster than it takes most people to commute to work. The average citizens (either in the United States or in the Soviet Union) do not think of war. They think of important things like house, family and work. And yet there are the American and Russian military forces whose job it is to think of nothing else but war. There are too many nuclear weapons and too many ways for them to be launched, shot, dropped or otherwise deployed against an opponent. It just does not seem likely that either Russia or America would deliberately launch a preemptive nuclear strike against the other. On the other hand, it is possible that we could accidentally find ourselves involved in a conflict—and there are just too many ways for an accident or incident to cause an escalation into a nuclear exchange (even the 'limited' exchange of tactical weapons). MAD cannot be an alternative for our future.

The second alternative is a negotiated deployment of similar defensive weapons and a simultaneous reduction of nuclear weapons. It must be understood that, because of the mistrust of one another, the United States and the Soviet Union will most likely never agree to a major reduction of nuclear arms unless they have both a strong defensive and offensive capability. This would be a sort of insurance policy for protection against any cheating by the opposition. The reality of the situation, however, is that spacebased defense systems as described are virtually undetectable until they are actually used. In the midst of an already marginal environment of fear, mistrust and suspicion, an undetectable capa-

bility will not do much to improve things. In effect then, this alternative is not much different than the existing SDI concept. The difference would hopefully be that we might avoid deployment concerns. It is readily admitted by proponents and opponents of SDI that the deployment of a system will be a tense time for all of the nations of the world.

The final alternative brings us back to our original questions about the SDI. This alternative is to simply eliminate nuclear weapons entirely. This alternative is also one of the long range goals of the SDI program. In his famous so-called 'Star Wars' speech, the president said, 'This could pave the way for arms control measures to eliminate the weapons themselves.' Is this at all possible?

Depending on who is counting, there are something more than 51,000 nuclear warheads in the world. These known warheads are distributed amongst five nations: China, France, the United Kingdom, the Soviet Union and the United States. Of these countries, fully 97 percent of the warheads belong to the United States and the Soviet Union. Again, depending on who is counting, both countries have about 25,000 warheads in each of their arsenals.

Reportedly, the smallest of these weapons is on the order of 10 times larger than today's most powerful conventional weapons. If we assume that these warheads have an average size in equivalent power of 200,000 pounds (one hundred kilotons) of TNT, and if we also assume there are six billion people on earth, that equates to almost one ton of TNT for each one of us.

When the very first atomic bomb was detonated at the Trinity Test Site in New Mexico, some of the scientists present regretted that they had been successful. Not too long

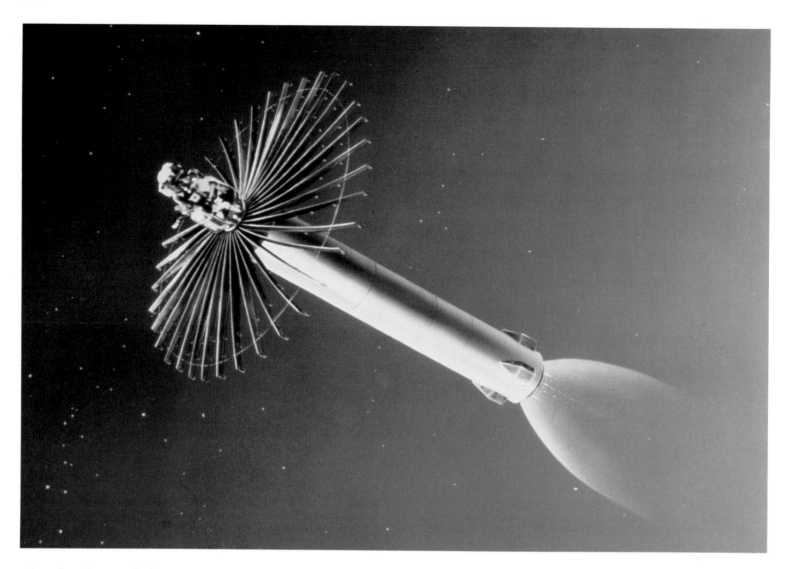

after that first explosion, a reporter asked one of the scientists what he thought of the results. His ominously prophetic response was, 'I am sure that at the end of the world, in the last few milliseconds of the Earth's existence, the last human will see what we saw.' The only real alternative we have is to find some way to completely eliminate nuclear weapons.

Throughout history people have accepted war as an inevitable event. It was commonly accepted that sooner or later there would be another war, but each of the recent world conflicts was thought of as the 'last war.' Whether we accept it or not, the world can no longer support a global conflict. We now have the capability to really make the next war the last war. Within the nuclear arsenals of the world, there is sufficient energy to kill us all.

Admittedly, nuclear war is not inevitable and the odds are long against such a conflict. However, time has a way of cutting down the odds. With the weapons available, we can say that someday there will be a nuclear exchange. This is what our military forces prepare for on an ongoing basis. We must constantly remind ourselves that a major nuclear exchange would essentially blanket the entire northern hemisphere with smoke and dust. According to the Nuclear Winter Theory, the surface of the earth would not see the sun for at least six months, and the temperature at the surface would drop well below freezing. After the clouds of war settle out of the atmosphere, the survivors of the war could expect to receive potentially fatal doses of ultraviolet radiation, because the ozone layer may well have been destroyed in the exchange of weapons. But—we may ask—won't the SDI prevent such a holocaust from happening? The answer is probably not.

The HOE vehicle looked like this conceptual sketch (*above*) when it closed in, 'umbrella spokes' extended, on its target. HOE targeting was so accurate that the spokes weren't needed to make contact. *At right:* Hiroshima, near ground zero, after 'Little Boy.'

The real threat of our future comes from our mind set—'war is inevitable and ultimately all can be solved through conflict' and 'all the nations of the world are most interested in protecting their vital interests.'

The ultimate cause of war is politics, but now science has given us the ultimate end to war. The flaw in our fabric of existence is that we are creative enough to build things with science, but not intelligent enough to learn how to live together.

If we finally do deploy the Strategic Defense Initiative, it will be a great success and a great failure at the same time. We will have found a way to push back the barriers of science and achieve technologies only dreamed of in the science fiction of years past. We however will also have failed to coexist peacefully with our neighbors. The deployment will be the triumph of technology and the admission of defeat. Albert Einstein once said, 'The unleashed power of the atom has changed everything except our way of thinking.' The research for SDI will take a few more years to develop. Hopefully, in that time we will not depend too much on technology, and we will find ways to bring about a negotiated, nonnuclear world peace. We should never forget that technology is not the only answer. We must always remember that no one nation, no matter how technologically advanced, can create world stability by itself.

SDI GLOSSARY

Acquisition
The process of detecting an object. An SDI acquisition sensor is designed to search a large area of space and distinguish potential targets from other objects against the background of space.

Airborne Optical Adjunct
A set of sensors designed to detect, track and discriminate incoming warheads in the terminal phase of flight. The sensors are typically optical or infrared devices carried aboard a high flying, long endurance aircraft.

Anti-Ballistic Missile (ABM)
A missile designed to intercept and destroy a strategic offensive ballistic missile or its reentry vehicle.

Anti-Satellite Weapon (ASAT)
A weapon designed to destroy satellites in space. The ASAT weapon may be ground-, air-, or spacebased.

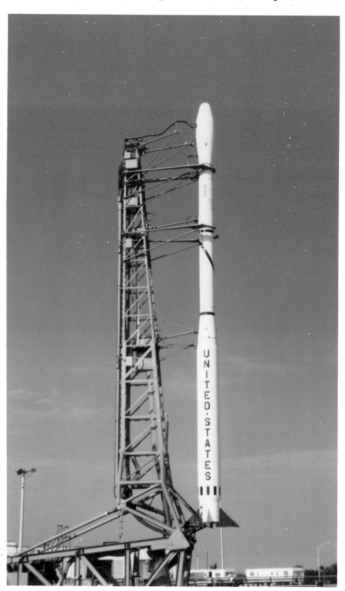

The target may be destroyed by a variety of methods based on either kinetic or directed-energy weapons.

Architecture
The description of the activities which are to be performed by the defensive system. The system elements required to perform the functions as envisioned.

Ballistic Missile
A vehicle propelled into space by rocket engines. The thrust is terminated at a predesignated time, after which the missile's reentry vehicles are released to free falling trajectories toward their targets.

Battle Management
The system of computers, communications and software designed to direct target selection, fire control, kill assessment and system command and control.

Birth-to-Death Tracking
The ability to track an object and its payload from the time it is launched until it is either intercepted or reaches its target.

Boost Phase
The first phase of a ballistic missile's trajectory. During this phase, usually lasting three to five minutes, the missile is powered by its engines and reaches an altitude of about 160 miles. At the end of the boost phase powered flight ends and the missile dispenses its reentry vehicles.

Booster
The engine portion of the missile which 'boosts' the payload and accelerates it from the surface of the earth into a ballistic missile trajectory.

Brightness
A term used to measure the intensity of the signature (infrared, for instance) of a target.

Bus
The platform which carries the warheads of a missile before they are released on their final trajectories. The bus is also referred to as a postboost vehicle.

Bus Deployment Phase
The portion of a missile flight during which multiple warheads are deployed on different paths toward different targets.

Chaff
Strips of metal foil, wire or metalized glass fiber which are used to reflect electromagnetic energy as a radar countermeasure.

Chemical Laser
A method of producing a laser beam using a chemical reaction to produce pulses of light.

Coherent Light
Light waves which are generated in phase—that is, of the same wave length.

Communication
The intercourse between two or more system assets such as ground sites, satellites etc.

Facing page, left—the Scout/ITV ASAT test target vehicle is positioned above its launch pad—and *right*—a US Pershing II IRBM blasts off from its base in Europe. *Above:* A Minuteman silo control panel. *Below:* The schema for a hypothetical naval battle.

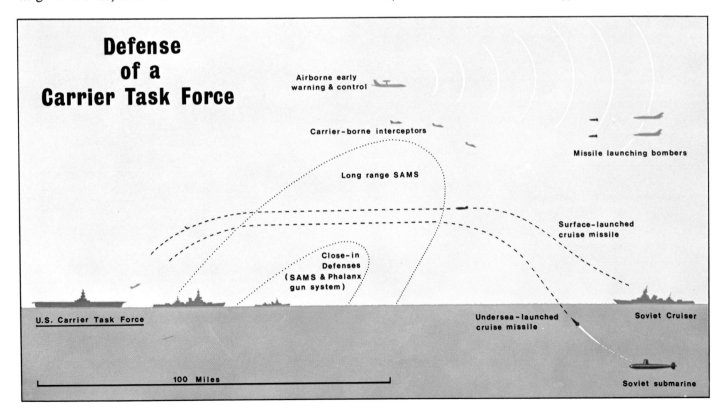

Continuous Wave Laser
A laser in which the coherent light is generated continuously rather than at fixed time intervals.

Decoy
A device constructed to 'look' and behave like a nuclear warhead. These are less costly than actual warheads and may be deployed in large numbers in an attempt to confuse defenses.

Directed Energy
Energy in the form of atomic particles, pellets or beams which can travel over long distances at near the speed of light.

Directed-Energy Weapon
A device that employs a tightly focused and precisely directed beam of very intense energy. This beam, traveling at nearly the speed of light, may be in the form of light or atomic particles.

Discrimination
The process of observing a set of threatening objects and determining which are real threats and which are decoys.

Distant Early Warning
The DEW Line is a defensive radar system set up to guard against air attack from over the North Pole.

Please note that the acronym **DEW** is used for the **Distant Early Warning System**—the United States' northern frontier radar defense warning system—and is also the acronym for **Directed Energy Weapon**—any of several devices which utilize an intensely focused beam of energy to disrupt a target. In this age of increasingly complex technology, this sort of thing is bound to happen. The intended usage of this acronym is therefore keyed to the context in which it appears—ie, the **DEW** *radar* does not destroy a target; it identifies a target; similarly, the **DEW** *weaponry* destroys a target; and so on.

Dynamic Reconfiguration
The changing of weapons and sensor systems to respond to the changing circumstances of an engagement, including orbital changes or the destruction of defense system assets.

Electromagnetic Gun
A device in which a projectile is accelerated by means of electromagnetic fields.

Electromagnetic Spectrum
The entire range of wave lengths or frequencies of electromagnetic radiation extending from gamma rays to the longest radio waves and including visible light.

Endoatmospheric
Considered to be within the atmosphere of the earth and at an altitude of less than 90 miles.

Engagement Time
The amount of time that a weapon requires in order to destroy a given target.

Exoatmospheric
Considered to be outside the atmosphere of the earth and at an altitude of more than 90 miles.

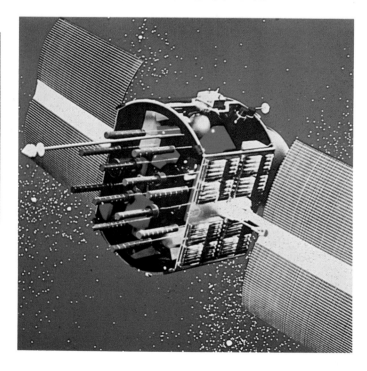

Fragment Clouds
Clusters of small objects placed in front of a target in space.

Free-electron Laser
A device in which energy from electrons is converted to produce a coherent pulse of laser light.

Gamma Ray
Electromagnetic radiation resulting from nuclear transitions.

Hardening
Measures which may be employed to render military assets less vulnerable.

Hypervelocity Gun
A device which can accelerate a projectile to an extraordinarily fast velocity (four to five miles per second).

Imaging
The process of identifying an object by obtaining a high-resolution 'picture' of it.

Infrared Sensor
A device used to detect the radiation from a cold body, such as a missile reentry vehicle.

Interception
The act of destroying a target.

Intercontinental Ballistic Missile (ICBM)
A missile with a range of between 3000 to 6000 miles. The term ICBM is only used for landbased systems in order to differentiate them from submarine-launched ballistic missiles.

Intermediate Range Ballistic Missile (IRBM)
A landbased ballistic missile with a range of between 2000 to 3000 miles.

Kinetic Energy
The energy of an object in motion.

Kinetic Energy Weapon (KEW)
A device which utilizes a nonexplosive projectile moving at very high speed in order to destroy a target on impact. The projectile may include a homing device to improve accuracy, or it may simply follow a preset trajectory. The projectile may be launched by means of a rocket, a conventional gun or a hypervelocity gun.

Laser
An acronym for light amplification by the stimulated emission of radiation. A beam of light is amplified when photons (quanta of light) are produced through the simultaneous stimulation of atoms, molecules or electrons.

Laser Designator
The use of a low power laser beam to illuminate a target so that a weapon equipped with a special tracker can 'home in' on a designated target. Low power lasers are also used in conjunction with groundbased lasers to

Both pages, top to bottom, left to right: Particles fired from a Kinetic Energy Weapon; the NASA Relay Communications Satellite; a NAVSTAR satellite; cutaway view of an ICBM silo complex at Vandenberg AFB; the DOD's 10 October 1985 laser tracking test.

188

Laser Imaging
A technique in which two or more lasers are used to illuminate a target so that a holographic image may be created.

Laser Tracker
The process of utilizing a laser to illuminate a target so that specialized sensors can detect the reflected laser light and track that target.

Layered Defense
A defensive system which consists of several sets of weapons and sensors which operate at different phases in the trajectory of a ballistic missile.

Leakage
The percentage of reentry vehicles that are able to pass through a defensive system toward a target.

Midcourse Phase
That portion of the trajectory of a ballistic missile between the boost and reentry phase. Usually lasting between 20 and 30 minutes, this phase of flight includes the separate trajectories of independent warheads and decoys.

Multiple Independently Targetable Reentry Vehicle (MIRV)
A group of two or more reentry vehicles which can be carried by a single ballistic missile and guided to separate targets.

Neutral Particle Beam
A beam of energetic neutral atoms accelerated, through the use of magnetic fields, to a velocity near the speed of light.

Nonnuclear Kill
A weapon which does not use a nuclear device to destroy a target.

Particle Beam
A stream of atoms or subatomic particles such as electrons, protons or neutrons, which are accelerated to nearly the speed of light.

Particle Beam Weapon
A device which relies on the technology of particle accelerators to emit beams of charged or neutral particles which travel at nearly the speed of light. Such a beam could theoretically destroy a target by several means including electronics disruption, softening of metal and explosive destruction.

Penetration Aids
Devices and methods which are employed as a way to defeat defenses by camouflage, deception, decoys or countermeasures.

Pointing and Tracking
Once a target is detected, it must be followed or 'tracked' until the target is intercepted.

Postboost Phase
The portion of a ballistic missile trajectory which follows the boost phase and precedes the midcourse phase.

Postboost Vehicle
The section of a ballistic missile that carries the reentry vehicles and has the capability to place each reentry vehicle on its final trajectory. Also referred to as a 'bus.'

Rail Gun
A weapon which uses electromagnetic fields to accelerate hypervelocity projectiles toward a target. Such projectiles have very high velocities, thereby reducing the lead angle required to shoot down (intercept) fast objects.

Realtime Protocols
Computer language devices designed to facilitate decisions as rapidly as input information is received.

Reentry Vehicle
That portion of a ballistic missile which carries a nuclear warhead. This vehicle is designed to re-enter the atmosphere in the terminal phase of its trajectory enroute to its target.

Repetitively Pulsed Laser
A beam which is propagated in short bursts rather than as a continuous beam. The free-electron laser generates a pulsed beam.

Responsive Threat
Offensive forces which have been modified in order to defeat a defensive theme.

Rocks
Kinetic energy devices which are propelled toward a target. So-called rocks have no internal electronics to track a target. Like bullets, they are aimed and propelled toward a target in a line-of-sight fashion.

Signal Processing
The capability of a computer system to receive and organize the data transmitted from many different sources.

Signature
The characteristic pattern of the target which is displayed by detection and identification equipment.

Smart Rocks
Kinetic energy projectiles which have homing, and possibly propulsion, devices incorporated.

Submarine-Launched Ballistic Missile (SLBM)
A submarine-based ballistic missile with a range of 2000 miles or less. The offensive advantage of these weapons is the elusiveness of the submarines carrying them.

Surveillance
Strategic information gathered by tactical observations, optical, infrared, radar and radiometric sensors.

Survivability
The capability of a system to avoid or withstand man-made hostile environments without suffering an irreversible impairment of its ability to accomplish its designated mission.

Terminal Phase
The final phase of a ballistic missile trajectory. During this phase, the warheads and penetration aids re-enter the atmosphere of the earth. This phase continues until the impact or interception of the missile occurs.

Threat Clouds
Dense concentration of both threatening and non-threatening objects. Defensive sensors must be capable of discriminating between threatening and nonthreatening objects.

Trajectory
The course or path of a ballistic missile, reentry vehicle, or decoys enroute from launch to designated target.

Vulnerability
The characteristics of a space system which can cause it to suffer degradation as a result of having been subjected to hostile environments.

X Ray
Electromagnetic radiation that is produced by bombarding a metallic target with fast electrons in a vacuum or by transition of atoms to lower energy status.

X Ray Beam
A power stream of electromagnetic energy which could be used to disrupt electronics, and perhaps to destroy ballistic missiles or reentry vehicles.

Opposite, left: The target vehicle for the 27 June 1986 FLAGE experiment rides under this US Navy F-4, and 30 seconds after its release, the FLAGE weapon, guided by built-in active millimeter wave radar and miniature steering rockets, destroyed this target. *Above:* A Polaris A-3 SLBM erupts from the *SSN Patrick Henry.*

INDEX

Above: This Minuteman missile shell fronts the Strategic Air Command world headquarters building near Omaha, Nebraska. This missile display is symbolic of the worldwide conventional and nuclear armaments force which SAC commands. *Overleaf:* The translucent globe *in the distance* is the beautiful and fragile planet Earth, as seen on Christmas Eve of 1968 by the Apollo 8 astronauts, as they orbited the Moon (which horizon is *in the foreground*). Peace on Earth may well have as much to do with the private heart of each man and woman—what we do, and why we do it—as the strategies and plotting which seem to be so sadly necessary in our present world.